Applied Statistics in Occupational Safety and Health

Second Edition

CHRISTOPHER A. JANICAK

GOVERNMENT INSTITUTES

An imprint of
THE SCARECROW PRESS, INC.
Lanham, Maryland • Toronto • Plymouth, UK

 **Government Institutes**

Published in the United States of America
by Government Institutes, an imprint of The Scarecrow Press, Inc.
A wholly owned subsidiary of
The Rowman & Littlefield Publishing Group, Inc.
4501 Forbes Boulevard, Suite 200
Lanham, Maryland 20706
http://www.govinstpress.com/

Estover Road, Plymouth PL6 7PY
United Kingdom

British Library Cataloguing in Publication Information Available

Library of Congress Cataloging-in-Publication Data

Janicak, Christopher A.
  Applied statistics in occupational safety and health / Christopher A. Janicak. — 2nd ed.
    p. cm.
  Includes bibliographical references and index.
  ISBN-13: 978-0-86587-169-4 (pbk. : alk. paper)
  ISBN-10: 0-86587-169-8 (pbk. : alk. paper)
  1. Industrial safety—Statistical methods. 2. Industrial hygiene—Statistical methods. 3. Research, Industrial. I. Title.
  T55.3.S72J36 2007
  363.11072—dc22   2006101616

Manufactured in the United States of America.

Contents

Preface   xi

1   Fundamentals of Statistics   1
      Statistics and Their Use in Safety   1
      Statistics Defined   2
      Common Terms and Notations   2
          Quantitative Data and Qualitative Data   3
      Statistical Notations   3
      Research Questions and Hypotheses   4
      Types of Studies   4
          Retrospective Studies   4
          Prospective Studies   5
          Experiments   5
      Statistical Samples versus Statistical Populations   5
      Bias   6
      Probability Sample Selection Procedures   6
          Random Samples   7
          Sampling Techniques   7
          Simple Random Samples   7
          Cluster Samples   8
          Stratified Random Samples   10
      Nonprobability Sample Selection Procedures   10
          Chunk Sampling   10
          Volunteer Samples   10
      Variables   10
          Dependent and Independent Variables   11
      Chapter Summary   11
      Chapter Review Exercises   12
2   Probability and Chance   15
      Probability   15
      Probability Rules   15

Simple Event Probabilities	16
Joint Event Probabilities	16
Compound Event Probabilities	17
Conditional Probabilities	18
Permutations, Ordered Combinations, and Combinations	19
Permutations	19
Ordered Combinations	20
Combinations	21
Binomial Probabilities	22
Binomial Probability Formula	22
Binomial Probability Example	22
Poisson Probability	23
Poisson Probability Formula	23
Poisson Probability Example	23
Chapter Summary	23
Chapter Review Exercises	24
3 Distributions	27
Statistical Distributions and Populations	27
Frequencies	27
Frequency Distribution Example	27
Histograms	28
Frequency Polygons	29
Percentages, Cumulative Percentages, and Percentiles	30
Normal Distribution	31
Binomial Distribution	32
Binomial Distribution Example	32
t Distribution	35
Chi-square Distribution	37
F Distribution	37
Chapter Summary	38
Chapter Review Exercises	38
4 Descriptive Statistics	39
Data Formats	39
Categorical Data	39
Ordinal Data	39
Interval Data	40
Ratio Data	40
Strength of the Data Formats	40
Measures of Central Tendency	41
Mean	41
Median	41
Mode	42
Measures of Variability	42
Range	42
Variance	43

Standard Deviation	44
Interquartile Range	44
z Scores	45
z Score Formula	45
z Score Problem	45
z Scores and Percentages of the Population	46
Confidence Intervals for Means	49
95% Confidence Intervals	49
99% Confidence Intervals	51
Interpreting Confidence Intervals	51
Chapter Summary	51
Chapter Review Exercises	52
5 Statistical Tests	**53**
Statistical Hypotheses	53
Inferential Statistical Testing	54
Type I and Type II Errors	54
α Levels	55
Statistical Power of a Test	55
Inferential Statistics Test Procedure	56
Developing a Statistical Hypothesis	56
Choosing the Appropriate Statistical Test or Procedure	56
Determining the Statistical Distribution	56
Determining Significance Levels	57
Formulating a Decision Rule	57
Running the Test	57
Formulating a Conclusion and Making a Decision	57
Chapter Summary	57
Chapter Review Exercises	58
6 Inferential Statistics for Means	**59**
z Tests	59
Test Assumptions	59
Hypothesis Construction	59
Determine Significance Levels	60
Using a *z* Table	60
Formulate a Decision Rule	61
z Test Formula	61
Conclusions	61
Example *z* Test Problem	61
t Tests	62
Test Assumptions	63
Hypothesis Construction	63
Determine Significance Levels	63
Formulate a Decision Rule	64
t Test Formula for a Single Mean	64
t Test Formula for Independent Groups	64

Conclusions	65
Example *t* Test Problem	65
Paired *t* Tests	66
Test Assumptions	66
Hypothesis Construction	67
Determine Significance Levels	67
Formulate a Decision Rule	67
Test Formula	67
Conclusions	68
Example Paired *t* Test Problem	68
One-way Analysis of Variance	69
Procedure Assumptions	70
Hypothesis Construction	70
Procedure Formulas	70
Hypothesis Construction	73
Formulate a Decision Rule	73
Calculate *F* Ratio	74
Conclusions	74
Post Hoc Procedures	74
Scheffe's Test	74
Calculate Scheffe's CD	75
Formulate a Decision Rule	75
Example ANOVA Problem	75
Formulate a Decision Rule	78
Calculate *F* ratio	78
Conclusions	78
Chapter Summary	78
Chapter Review Exercises	78
7 Correlation and Regression	81
Correlation	81
Pearson Correlation Coefficient	82
Spearman Rank-Order Correlation Coefficient	84
Phi Coefficient	85
Eta Coefficient	86
Point Biserial Correlation	87
Significance Testing for Correlation Coefficients	89
Regression	90
Assumptions	90
Formulas	90
Sample Problem	91
Chapter Summary	93
Chapter Review Exercises	93
8 Nonparametric Statistics	97
Underlying Assumptions Concerning Nonparametric Statistics	97
Chi-square Test for Goodness of Fit	97

Degrees of Freedom   97
Test Assumptions   98
Hypothesis Construction   98
Test Formula   98
Determine Critical Value   98
Sample Problem   98
χ^2 Test of Association   100
Degrees of Freedom   100
Expected Number of Cases   100
Test Assumptions   100
Hypothesis Construction   101
Test Formula   101
Sample Problem   101
Wilcoxon Rank-Sum Test   102
Test Assumptions   102
Hypothesis Construction   103
Test Formula   103
Sample Problem   103
Cochran's Q Test   105
Test Assumptions   105
Hypothesis Construction   105
Test Formula   106
Sample Problem   106
Chapter Summary   107
Chapter Review Exercises   108
9   Survey Research   109
Types of Survey Studies   109
Planning a Survey Study   109
Collection and Maintenance   109
Outline for Planning a Survey   110
Constructing the Instrument   113
Types of Survey Items   113
Forms of Questions   114
Unstructured Questions   114
Structured Questions   114
Rating Scales   115
Likert-type Scales   115
Semantic Differential Scales   116
Formatting Questionnaires for the Mail   116
Sound Survey Research Procedures   117
Measurable Objective   117
Representative Population   118
Match the Hypothesis to the Statistical Tests   118
Conduct Background Research   118
Instrument Validity and Reliability   118

Cover Letters and Instructions   119
Sampling for Surveys   119
Calculating Sample Sizes   120
Survey Research Limitations   120
Pilot Testing   120
Permission to Use Human Subjects   121
Chapter Summary   121
Chapter Review Exercises   121
10   Experimental Design   123
Experimental Design Uses   123
Research Hypotheses and Experimental Design   123
Dependent and Independent Variables   124
Types of Experimental Designs   124
One-way ANOVA   124
Completely Randomized Design   125
Randomized Block Design   125
Latin Square Design   125
Completely Randomized Factorial Design   126
Chapter Summary   126
Chapter Review Exercises   126
11   Presenting Research   129
Data Presentation for Safety Professionals   129
Displaying Descriptive Statistics   129
Displaying Tables   130
Bar Charts   130
Pie Charts   131
Presenting Inferential Statistics   132
z Tests and t Tests   132
One-way Analysis of Variance   132
Correlation Procedures   133
Regression Procedures   133
Nonparametric Procedures   133
Using Computer Software to Develop Presentations   133
Sample Data Analysis Using Microsoft Excel   134
Developing Presentations Using Microsoft Office   136
Chapter Summary   136
Chapter Review Exercises   136

Appendixes: Statistical Tables

Appendix A: Cumulative Distribution Function for the
Standard Normal Random Variable   138

Appendix B: Critical Values for the t Distribution   142

Appendix C: Critical Values for the Chi-square Distribution   144

Appendix D: Critical Values for the F Distribution   146

Appendix E: Table of Random Units   147

Glossary of Terms   149

References   155

Solutions to Selected Sample Problems   157

Index   181

About the Author   185

Preface

The major responsibilities of occupational safety and health professionals are to identify where problems exist and to develop interventions to solve those problems. The problem-identification process requires the safety professional to determine what the current situation is and compare it to what is acceptable. If the situation is unacceptable, intervention is required. The safety professional must then determine if the intervention is working. To meet these responsibilities, the safety professional must be able to collect data, analyze them, draw conclusions from them, and communicate the results to others.

This book provides the safety professional with the basic statistical and data analysis techniques that can be used to address some of the problems that he or she will encounter on a daily basis. It covers the data analysis process, from research design to data collection, analysis, reaching of conclusions, and presentation of the findings. At the end of each chapter, sample problems are provided to help users of this book learn to apply the information presented. Solutions to most problems appear at the back of the book.

Chapter 1 presents the more common terms and notation used in statistics. Proper design of research hypotheses and studies is described, as well as the procedures one should follow when selecting subjects for a study. A variety of sampling techniques are discussed, along with examples of appropriate uses of these sampling techniques.

Chapter 2 provides, in detail, the concepts of probability and chance, the underlying principles of statistical significance. Probability formulas are presented for simple, joint, compound, and conditional events. Binomial and Poisson probabilities that the safety professional may encounter in various statistical applications are also presented.

The different distributions that the results of statistical tests may assume are discussed in Chapter 3, as well as the procedures for constructing histograms and frequency polygons.

Chapters 4 through 8 discuss descriptive statistics, inferential statistics, and non-parametric statistics. These chapters discuss hypotheses testing using the various procedures and formulas, and also discuss determining the significance of the results of the test or procedure.

One of the most frequently used methods for obtaining data is the survey. Surveys are often one of the most incorrectly used methods, resulting in data that are unreliable or invalid. Chapter 9 discusses the proper way to conduct survey research, covering item development, sample selection, and survey research management.

Related to data collection and statistics is the field of experimental design. The researcher can use a variety of techniques and designs to collect data while controlling factors that may have an influence on the results. Chapter 10 provides a summary of various experimental designs that can be used in statistical research. While the reader of this book may not necessarily use all of the techniques, it is worth knowing how they are used since they are often discussed or mentioned in the literature.

With the research study complete, the safety professional must be capable of conveying the information to management and others in the field. Chapter 11 discusses the techniques and methodologies for presenting data. Proper formats for tables, graphs, and charts are discussed, as well as how to use Microsoft Office to analyze, summarize, and display the results.

CHAPTER 1

Fundamentals of Statistics

Statistics and Their Use in Safety

This book was written with the safety professional in mind. Safety professionals encounter statistics in the literature they read, such as business reports, and so on, and may be required to present findings or make decisions based on data analyses. Statistics can be used to justify the implementation of a program, identify areas that need to be addressed, or justify the impact that various safety programs have on losses and accidents. Safety professionals also use a variety of data in their day-to-day work. For example, the number of accidents reported in a given time frame may give an indication of the performance of a safety program; the amount of money paid out in losses may indicate the severity of the accidents. And safety professionals are required to interpret existing studies and statistics. They must be able to determine whether the results and conclusions are valid and whether the procedures have been used in an appropriate manner.

In process safety management, the identification and evaluation of hazardous operations can be directed back to the probabilities of failures of the components, subsystems, and systems in question. Statistical analyses are necessary to make these determinations. In the workplace, exposure to various chemicals and materials can result in increased risk for illness, which again is measured in terms of probabilities.

This book is designed to provide the people that are preparing to become practicing safety professionals or those already practicing in the field with the basic methods and principles necessary to apply statistics properly. It presents the reader with descriptive statistical concepts and how these concepts can be used to summarize data. Inferential statistics for parametric and nonparametric procedures will be presented using a systematic approach. Although the tests and hypotheses are different, the same basic steps can be followed for both types of procedures.

Statistics Defined

The word *statistic* has two different meanings (Kuzma 1992, 2). First, a *statistic* can be a numerical term that summarizes or describes a sample. Statistics are obtained from samples and, if used correctly, can describe a population. This is the case with inferential statistics.

Second, *statistics* can be defined as the science that deals with the collection, tabulation, and systematic classification of data. Statistics as a field of study uses mathematics and probability to formulate, describe, and test research hypotheses. It consists of a set of rules and procedures for measuring and compiling information obtained from observations.

The field of statistics can be broadly classified into two major areas: descriptive statistics and inferential statistics (Horvath 1974, 5).

Descriptive statistics consists of the techniques that are used to summarize and describe quantitative measurements taken for a population or sample. Examples of descriptive statistics include means, percentages, and frequencies. Descriptive statistics are used to describe the characteristics of a sample and are usually used in the first stages of data analysis.

Inferential statistics, on the other hand, uses the results from a subset or sample to infer the results to a larger group or population. Statistical procedures allow us to make this jump from results from a smaller group to a larger population by incorporating degrees of probability into the results. If done properly, the researcher can take measurements from a sample and, with a certain degree of confidence, be assured of similar results to those that would have been found if the entire population had been measured. The field of statistics provides the rules and procedures that must be followed to be able to accurately generalize the results from a sample to a much larger population.

Common Terms and Notations

The field of statistics uses some common terminology and symbols. Statistical notation uses Greek letters and algebraic symbols to convey meaning about the procedures that one should follow to complete a particular test. For the most part, the letters and symbols are consistent in the discipline. The first major delineation between the symbols occurs when the data being analyzed represent a population or a sample. A population signifies that one has measured a characteristic for everyone or everything that belongs to that particular group. For example, if one wishes to measure a characteristic on the population defined as safety managers, one would have to go and get a measure of that characteristic for every safety manager possible. In many cases, measuring a population is quite difficult, if not impossible. In statistics, we most often obtain data from a sample and use the results from the sample to describe the whole population. In the example described above, the researcher may go and measure a characteristic from a selected group of safety managers. When the researcher does this, he is using a sample.

A member of a population or a sample is referred to as a subject or a case. As will be discussed later in this book, there are statistical methods for determining how many cases must be selected to have a sound study. For each case, the measurements taken for the purposes of statistical analysis are considered data. Data are the recorded observations gathered for the purposes of a statistical study.

QUANTITATIVE DATA AND QUALITATIVE DATA

In a study, the researcher will be collecting a variety of information and taking many measurements for data analysis. The measurements can be classified as either qualitative or quantitative (Witte and Witte 1997, 5). If the measurements deal with characteristics about the individual or subject, they are qualitative. Additional examples of qualitative measures include the gender of a person or the color of a sign. For the purposes of data analysis, qualitative measures are coded with numbers. For example, 1 may represent "male" and 2 may represent "female."

Quantitative measures are measures that describe a characteristic in terms of a number. Quantitative measures can be the age of a person measured in years or the number of accidents an organization had over the previous year.

Statistical Notations

When a statistician uses notations to describe the statistical tests, procedures, or results, the format of the notation signifies whether the statistician is dealing with a population or a sample. Statistical notation for a population is written using Greek letters, while statistical notation for a sample is written using English letters. Table 1.1 summarizes some of the more common statistical terms that will be used in this book.

There are also statistical terms that signify mathematical procedures to be performed on the data. For example, the Greek letter Σ instructs the statistician to sum or add up the terms. Some of the more common procedural terms used in this book are in Table 1.2.

Table 1.1.   Statistical Terms Used in This Text

Statistical Term	Population Notation	Sample Notation
Mean	—	x
Standard deviation	σ	s
Variance	σ^2	s^2
Number of cases	N	n
Raw number or value	X	x
Correlation coefficient	R	r

Table 1.2.   Statistical Symbols and Procedures Used in This Text

Symbol	Procedure	Example
Σ	Sum of	Σx – add up all raw numbers
$\lvert x \rvert$	Absolute value of x	$\lvert -5 \rvert = 5$
$n!$	Factorial of n	$5! = 5 \times 4 \times 3 \times 2 \times 1$

Research Questions and Hypotheses

All statistical tests and procedures begin with a question the researcher wishes to answer. The questions can be as simple as "What is the average age of the injured person?" to "Is there a significant relationship between exposure to a chemical and cancer?" The questions can be answered with descriptive statistics or can be tested with inferential statistics. When researchers ask a question that is tested with statistics, they have developed a hypothesis. Researchers use statistics to confirm or reject the hypothesis being tested.

Types of Studies

To conduct a research study using statistics, the researcher must collect data, develop a model, and then determine the intervention needed to prevent or correct a problem. The model is what we use to determine what decisions we must make concerning the problem at hand. If the data do not support the model, then we must go back and develop a new model. We can go two directions in regard to models and observations. First, we can make our observations and then create the model to fit what we have observed. If we do this, we are engaged in what is called *inductive research*. An example of inductive research would be a safety manager who is experiencing a number of hand injuries in the plant. The manager collects the data on this problem. Using the data, the manager develops a model that could be used to describe why these accidents are occurring.

The other form of research is called *deductive research*. When a person is engaged in deductive research, he or she develops a model and then tests it using data collected from the observations. Examples of deductive research are in various types of inventories. The manager formulates a model to explain why there is an increase in accidents, then collects the data and tests the model he created.

RETROSPECTIVE STUDIES

Studies can also be classified according to their overall framework. A retrospective study examines past events to determine the factors that influenced the events (Kuzma 1992, 6). The accidents occurred in the past, and the investigator looks back in time to reach conclusions about the events that led up to the accidents. In a typical accident analysis, the investigator examines accidents that occurred, and based on that information identifies areas that should be addressed.

PROSPECTIVE STUDIES

Prospective studies examine the outcomes of events that occur in the future. In a prospective study, the data are collected and analyzed, and conclusions about how the results should turn out in the future are formulated (Kuzma 1992, 6). An example of a prospective analysis would be one in which the safety professional institutes an accident prevention program and then monitors losses into the future to determine the effectiveness of the intervention.

EXPERIMENTS

An experiment is another format for a research study. Conducting experiments using control groups is a method used when one wishes to show cause-and-effect relationships (Horvath 1974, 133). The main features of an experiment are the presence of an experimental group, a control group, and random selection of subjects. The experimental group is the group that receives the treatment, while the control group receives no treatment. Assuming random selection and placement into these two groups, comparisons are made between the two groups and any differences noted are assumed to be due to the treatment.

Within the family of experiments, several different methods can be used to conduct a study. These include blind studies and double blind studies. In a blind study, the subjects do not know if they are really receiving the treatment. They may be receiving a placebo. A placebo is a treatment that has no effects on the subjects. A placebo is used to ensure that the treatment is the actual cause for the differences between the control and experimental groups and not a result of being treated or part of the study.

In a double blind study, neither the person providing the treatment nor the subjects know if they are really receiving a treatment. This type of study is used to ensure there is neither conscious nor unconscious bias by the person receiving the treatment as well as the person providing the treatment or measuring results. What can happen is that if the person taking measurements knows that the subject is receiving a particular treatment, they may subconsciously begin to "see" results that really are not there, mostly because they are expecting the results.

Statistical Samples versus Statistical Populations

A *statistical sample* represents the set of outcomes that are being measured for the purposes of analyses. For example, a safety manager wants to determine if employees are following the established procedures correctly. One way of collecting this information is to draw a sample of employees and observe their performance. A sample is a subset of the total population. When we examine a sample statistically, we make some inferences about that sample in terms of its representativeness of the population.

A *population* is the all-inclusive group of subjects that have the characteristics we are interested in observing. For example, the safety manager that wishes to conduct a study on safe job behaviors for a company would have to observe every employee at the company. The population would be defined as workers at company XYZ. Because this can be very tedious and time consuming, one can select a subset of the population that has the same characteristics as the population. When done properly, the researcher may be able to assume that the results obtained from the sample are representative of the population.

Bias

Bias in a study is a systematic error that may taint the results of the study. A bias in the selection process, for example, can result in a group of people that for whatever reason are not considered to be representative of the population. Sampling biases can result due to clerical errors, inadequate data, and procedural errors. Sampling bias is the difference between the sample result obtained and the sample that would have been obtained had better sampling procedures been used. Sampling biases that tend to be more systematic, occur in patterns, or are repetitive are more likely to distort the obtained results. Nonsampling biases can also be present in sampling. These biases include errors in data processing, item writing, interpretation, key punching, and so on. Additional examples of bias are listed below (Kuzma 1992, 270):

- *Observer bias*: The observer or interviewer is fully aware of the potential outcomes. He or she may consciously or subconsciously attribute the characteristics to the subject.
- *Sampling bias*: The researcher may not get a truly representative sampling of the population.
- *Dropout bias*: A certain proportion of the sample may drop out due to various reasons, and those who drop out may be different from those who continue.
- *Memory bias*: Relying on memory may change perceptions about the responses. The more recent past is remembered better than the distant past.
- *Participant bias*: This may occur when the subject has knowledge of whether he is in a control or experimental group.

Probability Sample Selection Procedures

Because it would be extremely time-consuming and in many cases impossible to obtain data from every member of a population, researchers use the results from samples to describe or infer the results to the larger populations. However, the researcher must be careful to ensure that the results obtained from the sample are truly representative of the population. Any differences between what the researcher would have obtained from the population and the obtained sample results are referred to as error. It is almost impossible to eliminate these differences or error from the results. The best that the researcher can do is minimize the error to such a level that the sample results are not significantly different from the population results.

RANDOM SAMPLES

One way of trying to ensure that the sample has similar characteristics to the population and to minimize the error is to randomly select the subjects. For a sample to be random, each person in the population should have an equal chance of being selected to be included in the study. Random selection is one of the best ways of ensuring there that are no biases in the method used to select the subjects to participate in the study.

SAMPLING TECHNIQUES

As previously discussed, one method for reducing the possibility of sampling biases in the sample is with a random sampling technique. If the subjects are randomly sampled, the chances of selecting subjects with characteristics that do not match the population are reduced. Biases arise in the sampling technique when the researcher systematically over- or underselects people with a particular characteristic. There are several random sampling techniques that can be used to reduce the chances for bias. These techniques are the simple random sample, the stratified random sample, and the cluster sample (Backstrom and Hursh-Cesar 1981, 57–63).

SIMPLE RANDOM SAMPLES

A simple random sample may be used if the population being selected from is small and the researcher is capable of enumerating each subject. The process of conducting a simple random sample selection is as follows:

1. Number each of the subjects in the population.
2. Determine the number of subjects necessary to complete the study.
3. Using a random numbers table, identify the cases that should be included in the sample. There are a variety of sources for random numbers tables, ranging from statistical books to extensive books of random numbers tables. A random numbers table is shown in Appendix A.

Using a Random Numbers Table

If an investigator has 100 subjects in the population and wishes to randomly select 15 to be included in the sample, he begins at the top of the random numbers table and reads the first three digits in the first number. If the digits coincide with a numbered case in the population, then that subject is included in the sample. If the digits do not represent a case in the population, then the investigator continues down the list. The investigator continues down the list of random numbers, identifying the cases. When 15 subjects have been identified with the table, the selection process ends. An excerpt from a random numbers table is presented below (see Table 1.3) and a random numbers table is presented in Appendix A.

Random Numbers Table Example

An investigator wishes to randomly select 10 subjects from a group of 100 using a random numbers table. The investigator assigns each subject in the group a number from 1 to 100. Since the maximum number of digits in a subject's assigned number can be is three ("100" has three digits to it), the investigator reads the three digits from the first random number and determines if a subject is assigned that number. The investigator can choose the first three digits or the last three digits from the random number; it makes no difference as long as there is consistency in the selection. In this example, the investigator decides to use the last three digits. Starting at row 1, column 1, the random number 10480 has the sequence 480 as the last three digits. No one in the sample has been assigned a number 480, so the investigator goes to the next column to random number 15011. The last three digits are 011, which represents the subject assigned number 11. This person is selected to be in the group. The investigator continues across the first row until he reaches column 14, then proceeds to row 2 in column 1, and continues in this manner until 10 subjects have been identified. Keep in mind that the investigator also could have gone down the first column until the end and then proceeded to column 2 and down. The selection process would be considered random as long as the same pattern is followed throughout the selection process. If a random number comes up and the subject with that number has already been selected, the investigator will skip that number and continue until the number of desired subjects has been identified.

CLUSTER SAMPLES

A cluster sample is used when the researcher wishes to select a representative sample from geographic areas. The researcher must know the data being analyzed and know that there may be geographic differences in the way the subjects may respond to a particular research item. With this in mind, the researcher establishes a selection process to ensure the selection of representative numbers of people from the various geographic areas. A cluster sampling technique is used when researchers perform large-scale surveys and wish to get a representative sample of the beliefs of the nation as a whole. If there is reason to believe that results would vary according to geographic regions, the researcher would first divide the country into regions and then randomly select a certain number of subjects from each region.

Table 1.3. Excerpt from a Random Numbers Table

	(1)	(2)	(3)	(4)	(5)	(6)	(7)	(8)	(9)	(10)	(11)	(12)	(13)	(14)
1	10480	15011	01536	02011	81647	91646	69179	14194	62590	36207	20969	99570	91291	90700
2	22368	46573	25595	85393	30995	89198	27982	53402	93965	34091	52666	19174	39615	99505
3	24130	48360	22527	97265	76393	64809	15179	24830	49340	32081	30680	19655	63348	58629
4	42167	93093	06243	61680	07856	16376	39440	53537	71341	57004	00849	74917	97758	16379
5	37570	39975	81837	16656	06121	91782	60468	81305	49684	60672	14110	06927	01263	54613
6	77921	06907	11008	42751	27756	53498	18602	70659	90655	15053	21916	81825	44394	42880
7	99562	72905	56420	69994	98872	31016	71194	18738	44013	48840	63213	21069	10634	12952
8	96301	91977	05463	07972	18876	20922	94595	56869	69014	60045	18425	84903	42508	32307
9	89579	14342	63661	10281	17453	18103	57740	84378	25331	12566	58678	44947	05585	56941
10	85475	36857	43342	53988	53060	59533	38867	62300	08158	17983	16439	11458	18593	64952

STRATIFIED RANDOM SAMPLES

In a stratified random sample, the researcher anticipates that there may be differences in the results based on the subjects' membership in a particular group. With this in mind, the researcher divides the population into the various groups, and then a random sample is taken from each group. This procedure is used to ensure adequate representation from overpopulated and underpopulated groups. For example, an investigator performing a study in a facility about safety concerns in a plant had reason to believe that there would be differences in the safety concerns from department to department. The investigator first identified the subjects in each of the departments, then randomly selected a certain number of subjects from each area.

Nonprobability Sample Selection Procedures

Another form of sampling is referred to as nonprobability sampling. With these sampling techniques, there is a lack of randomness in the selection process and because of this lack of randomness, the results obtained from such a sample cannot be expected to be representative of the total population. Some examples of these selection techniques include chunk sampling and volunteer sampling (Backstrom and Cesar-Hursh 1981, 64–65).

CHUNK SAMPLING

In chunk sampling, the researcher selects people that happen to be present in a particular location at a particular time. This is most commonly seen when a reporter stops the first ten people that pass by.

VOLUNTEER SAMPLES

In a volunteer sample, the participants volunteer to participate in the study. An example of a volunteer sample is when a local television station asks people to call in with their vote. The people voluntarily provide their input to the study. Typically, the volunteers are strongly for the subject in question or strongly against it. Those that are considered middle-of-the-road do not typically volunteer their participation and thus are underrepresented.

Variables

With the sample selected, the researcher must decide which types of measurements will be necessary to obtain the information necessary. These characteristics or measurements are considered variables. A *variable* is any measurement that can have a potential range of values. A researcher who wishes to determine the average number of lost workdays per employee must count the number of days lost. This would be considered one variable.

DEPENDENT AND INDEPENDENT VARIABLES

Variables can be further classified into dependent and independent variables (Witte and Witte 1997, 7). Proper distinction between the two becomes important when performing statistical procedures such as correlations and regressions. A *dependent variable* is a variable that can be influenced or changed by other variables under study. An *independent variable* is a variable that measures characteristics that cannot be influenced or changed.

For example, an investigator wishes to determine if a relationship exists between a person's age and the number of days it takes him or her to recuperate from an injury. The investigator must measure the age of the person and the number of days the person was away from work due to an injury. In this case, it can be assumed that the person's age cannot be influenced by the number of days he or she missed work. The person's age is the independent variable. It is quite possible that the older the person is, the longer it may take that person to recover from an injury. Because the number of days the person missed work could be influenced by age, the number of days is considered the dependent variable.

The investigator must know, for various statistical tests, which variable is being influenced by what. It is important to note that dependent and independent variables can change from study to study. A particular variable may not always be independent or dependent. It depends on the statistical study at the time the variable is being used.

Chapter Summary

The first step in statistical analysis is to determine the framework for the analysis that will be necessary to answer the questions at hand. This can range from descriptive analyses to hypothesis testing. The research framework is dependent on the statistical questions and hypotheses. Major frameworks for research include retrospective studies, prospective studies, and experiments. Each has its own unique characteristics and desired outcomes. Formulating the proper research questions that need to be answered will assist the researcher in choosing the proper framework.

Before researchers can begin to use various statistical procedures and tests, they must determine what sources would best provide them the data for their analyses. The sample must be selected in a manner that ensures that it is representative of the population and free from biases. The sample selection process requires researchers to have background information about the data they are collecting and the possible factors that influence the results of the data. Using this information, a selection process should be selected and utilized.

The next step is to identify the variables that must be used to obtain the data necessary to complete the analysis. Identifying the variables and the methods for measuring them will allow the researcher to select the proper statistical procedures and tests. Characteristics about the variables may include the dependence of variables on one another and the best ways to measure the data.

Chapter Review Exercises

1. Describe the differences between a retrospective study, a prospective study, and an experiment.
2. Describe the differences between an independent variable and a dependent variable.
3. Describe the situations in which a researcher would use a simple random sample versus a cluster sample and a stratified random sample.
4. In each of the following cases, identify the dependent variable and the independent variable:

   grade on exam   hours studied
   training programs conducted   accident frequency
5. Define the following terms:

   bias   placebo
   variable   population
   statistics   double blind study
6. A researcher wishes to show that a particular drug really works. What must the researcher do to show cause and effect?
7. A researcher wishes to conduct a survey to identify people's perceptions of the economy in the United States. What type of sampling technique would be most appropriate and why?
8. The researcher wishes to perform a simple random sample selection using 100 people from a population of 1,000. Describe the process the researcher should go through to complete this task.
9. Provide an example of a study in which the researcher will use each of the following sampling techniques:

   chunk   cluster sample
   volunteer   simple random sample
   stratified random sample
10. For each of the following examples, provide the best format for a research study:

    A researcher wishes to identify past accident trends for an organization.

    A researcher wishes to determine if back belts really work.

    Researchers wish to set up a study wherein they measure performance in such a manner that their potential biases do not affect the outcomes.
11. When a researcher makes an observation and then creates a model to match it, the type of research is

    a. an experiment
    b. inductive research

    c. deductive research

    d. survey research

12. A researcher designed a study with a treatment group and a control group. This type of research is

    a. an experiment

    b. inductive research

    c. deductive research

    d. survey research

13. A researcher enumerated the sample, then used a table to select the cases. The type of sample selected is a

    a. cluster sample

    b. simple random sample

    c. chunk sample

    d. strata sample

14. The sampling method that accounts for geographic differences in the population is a

    a. cluster sample

    b. simple random sample

    c. chunk sample

    d. strata sample

15. An example of a nonprobability sample is a

    a. cluster sample

    b. simple random sample

    c. chunk sample

    d. strata sample

16. Define the dependent and independent variables of a hypothetical study.

17. A researcher wishes to randomly select five subjects from a population of 1,000 using a simple random selection. Using the random numbers table in Appendix A, identify the first five subjects that would be in the sample. Describe the process used to perform this selection.

18. Compare and contrast chunk sampling and stratified random sampling.

19. A safety manager wishes to evaluate the effectiveness of back belts in the workplace. Describe the dependent and independent variables one may use in a study such as this.

20. Describe the differences between a population and a sample. Give examples of each.

CHAPTER 2

Probability and Chance

Probability

Probability is the likelihood that an event will occur (Witte and Witte 1997, 190). In statistics, a researcher assumes that the likelihood a particular event has of occurring is due totally to chance. If the likelihood of obtaining a set of results totally due to chance is remote, the statistician may conclude that the results are statistically significant. (It is important to note that probability and possibility are two different concepts. Possibility determines whether an event can occur or not; probability is the likelihood or chance that it will.) One can determine probabilities for events or occurrences, and one can determine probabilities for analysis outcomes. To determine the probability of an event, the researcher determines the likelihood that it will occur. For studies, the statistician determines the likelihood of obtaining the results. If they are remote, then the study is considered to be significant.

Probabilities are determined for events. An event is an occurrence of any type. The letter P is used to signify probability and letters A, B, C, etc. are used to identify different events. Using this system, P_A represents the probability of event A. The term P_B represents the probability of event B, which is a different event compared with event A. Probability values are derived as decimal values, converted to a percentage and read as such. An obtained probability value of .05 is equivalent to a 5% probability.

Probability Rules

There are some rules that apply to the concepts of probabilities that allow a person to manipulate and interpret the results (Hays 1988, 22–25). For every event A, there is also a complementary event Å, read as not A. The sum of events A and Å is 1.00. This is the rule of complementary probability. The rule of probability range states that the probability of an event must be between 0 and 1.00.

SIMPLE EVENT PROBABILITIES

In a simple event probability, the researcher compares the number of times an event occurred to the total number of possible outcomes.

Simple Event Formula

The formula for calculating simple event probabilities is as follows (Hays 1988, 27):

$$P_A = \frac{\text{Number of wanted events}}{\text{Total number of possible events}}$$

Simple Event Example

An example of a simple event probability would be to determine the probability of any one component in a box being damaged if the safety manager found 15 damaged components out of 500 in a box. Using the formula for simple events, P_A represents the probability of selecting a bad component. The probability is a ratio between the number of events that fit the needs of the researcher (in this example the number of bad components) and the total number of events possible (in this case the total number of chips).

$$P_A = 15/500 = .03, \text{ or a 3\% chance of selecting a bad component}$$

JOINT EVENT PROBABILITIES

A joint event is an event about which the researcher can ask the question "What is the probability of event A and event B occurring at the same time?" To determine this, the researcher must multiply the probability of the independent events together.

Joint Event Formula

The formula for determining joint probabilities is as follows (Hays 1988, 37):

$$P_{A \text{ and } B} = P_A \times P_B$$

Joint Event Example

A safety manager was determining the probability of failure of a piece of equipment that uses two redundant switches. In order for a failure to occur to the system, both switches had to fail at the same time. The probability of failure for the system can be determined by multiplying the probability of failure of switch A and switch B. Assuming both switches have a probability of failure of .10, what is the probability of failure for the system?

$$P_{A \text{ and } B} = P_A \times P_B$$

$P_{A \text{ and } B} = (.10 \times .10) = .01$, or a 1% chance of system failure due to a failure of both switches

COMPOUND EVENT PROBABILITIES

Sometimes one must determine the probability of the occurrence of multiple events in a situation. However, instead of determining the failure due to all events occurring at the same time, a person may wish to determine the occurrence of one or more events at a time. These probabilities are referred to as compound probabilities. The overall probability of a compound event is determined by summing the individual event probabilities together, keeping in mind that the sum of all events must not exceed 1.00. The term *or* represents addition in compound probabilities.

Another decision the statistician must make concerns the mutual exclusiveness of the individual events. When two events are determined to be mutually exclusive, only one event can occur at a time. Another way of stating this is that the occurrence of one event excludes the occurrence of the second event. This becomes critical in compound event calculations.

An example that demonstrates the effects of mutual exclusiveness can be shown using a deck of cards. A statistician wishes to determine the probability of selecting a king or a red card from a deck of cards. Using the formula for a compound event, the statistician would add the probability of selecting a red card to the probability of selecting a king. The probability of selecting a red card is 26/52 or 50% and the probability of selecting a king is 4/52 or 8%. Addition of the two probabilities yields 58%. However, because these events are not mutually exclusive, a problem arises because the statistician is counting the two red kings twice (see Table 2.1). If the events are not mutually exclusive, meaning both events can occur at the same time (drawing one card that is both a red card and a king), then the statistician must subtract out the probability of both events occurring at the same time. The compound event formula provides for this correction. The correct probability for selecting a red card or a king would be as follows:

$$P_{\text{king}} + P_{\text{red card}} - P_{\text{king and a red card}}$$

$$(4/52) + (26/52) - (2/52) = .54 \text{ or } 54\%$$

Compound Event Formula

The formula for a compound event is as follows (Horvath 1974, 95–97):

$$P_{A \text{ or } B} = P_A + P_B - P_{A \times B}$$

Table 2.1.   Compound Probability Example

Red Cards		Kings
Ace of hearts	Ace of diamonds	King of hearts
2 of hearts	2 of diamonds	King of diamonds
3 of hearts	3 of diamonds	King of spades
4 of hearts	4 of diamonds	King of clubs
5 of hearts	5 of diamonds	
6 of hearts	6 of diamonds	
7 of hearts	7 of diamonds	
8 of hearts	8 of diamonds	
9 of hearts	9 of diamonds	
10 of hearts	10 of diamonds	
Jack of hearts	Jack of diamonds	
Queen of hearts	Queen of diamonds	
King of hearts	King of diamonds	

Compound Event Example

A loss control consultant was provided with loss data for a client. In one year there were 250 fires, the primary causes of which were determined to be smoking in 108 cases, cooking equipment in 95 cases, arson in 12 cases, and unknown origin in 35 cases. The loss control consultant would like to know what the probability is of selecting a fire claim from the group with a primary cause of either smoking or arson. Because the consultant is determining a probability of "one or the other," he will be determining a compound event. The consultant must then determine whether or not the events are mutually exclusive. To do this he must answer the question "Can one claim, when selected, have both characteristics present? In this example, can one claim have a primary cause of smoking and a primary cause of arson?" The consultant determines that this is not possible; therefore the events are mutually exclusive and the probability of both events occurring at the same time is zero.

$$P_{\text{smoking or arson}} = P_{\text{smoking}} + P_{\text{arson}} - P_{\text{smoking and arson}}$$

$P_{\text{smoking or arson}} = (108/250) + (12/250) - 0 = .48$, or 48% chance of selecting a claim with smoking or arson as the primary cause

CONDITIONAL PROBABILITIES

In a conditional probability, some condition or restriction is placed on the sample that is being used to determine the probability (Witte and Witte 1997, 193–94). The total size of the sample is reduced in some way. Then the probability of an event is determined using the subset of the total population. In conditional probabilities, the symbol "/" represents the phrase "given the fact." A conditional probability of A/B is read as "given the fact that B has occurred, what is the probability of event A?"

Conditional Probability Formula

The formula for calculating a conditional probability is as follows (Witte and Witte 1997, 193–94):

$$P_{A/B} = \frac{P_{A \text{ and } B}}{P(B)}$$

Conditional Probability Example

A safety manager wanted to determine the probability of having a lost workday charged to a worker because of a back injury. The safety manager determined that for the 87 claims of all types reported in one year, 18 involved lost workdays. Of the 87 reported claims, 23 were for back injuries, and of these 23 cases, 14 resulted in lost workdays. The safety manager wishes to determine the probability of a lost workday case if the case was the result of a back injury.

　　To determine this, the safety manager first determines the probability of a back injury case from all reported cases. In this example, the probability of having a back injury case reported is 23/87, or 26%. Next, the safety manager must determine the probability of a case that is a back injury and a lost workday case. The probability is 14/87, or 16%. Using the conditional probability formula, the following was derived:

$$P_{\text{a lost workday case/a back injury was reported}} = \frac{P_{\text{a lost workday case and a back injury case}}}{P_{\text{a back injury was reported}}}$$

$$P_{\text{a lost workday case/a back injury was reported}} = \frac{.16}{.26} = .61, \text{ or a } 61\% \text{ chance}$$

Therefore, given the fact that the case reported was a back injury, there is a 61% chance that the case is a lost workday case.

Permutations, Ordered Combinations, and Combinations

In the examples presented thus far, the total number of possible events has been provided or easily determined by counting the total number of cases in the sample or population. In some situations, the total number of possible outcomes must be calculated. Permutations, combinations, and factorials can be used to calculate the total number of possible outcomes.

PERMUTATIONS

A factorial is represented by the sign "!" and represents a multiplication of values. For example, the term 6! is read as 6 factorial. It is represented by the equation $6 \times 5 \times 4$

Table 2.2.   Letter Combinations

ABCD	ABDC	ACBD	ACDB	ADBC	ADCB
BACD	BADC	BCAD	BCDA	BDAC	BDCA
CABD	CADB	CBAD	CBDA	CDAB	CDBA
DABC	DACB	DBAC	DBCA	DCAB	DCBA

× 3 × 2 × 1, or a value of 720. The term 3! is represented by the equation 3 × 2 × 1, or a value of 6. Factorials can be used to determine the total number of combinations in which a set of items can be arranged using all available items. For example, how many combinations can the letters A, B, C, and D be placed into using all available letters? Because there are 4 letters, we calculate 4!, which gives us an answer of 24, that is, 24 combinations using all 4 letters. The letter combinations are displayed in Table 2.2.

If a person placed 4 pieces of paper into a hat with the letters A, B, C, and D on them and then drew each slip out, what is the probability of pulling the pieces out in the exact order of BCAD? Using a simple event-probability formula, the statistician sees that the combination of BCAD occurs once and there are 24 possible combinations to choose from, so the probability of selecting the 4 pieces of paper in that exact order is 1/24, or 4%.

ORDERED COMBINATIONS

In some situations, the total number of items used to develop the combinations does not equal the total number of items available. Using the data from above, the statistician has 4 letters to choose from but instead of using all 4 letters, he decides to choose 3-letter combinations, and a different order of letters represents a different combination. Because the number of items selected is less than the number available and because a different order represents a different combination (A, B, C is different from B, C, A), the statistician must derive an ordered combination. Two pieces of information are needed to calculate the ordered combination. They are n, the number of items available, and r, the number of items selected at one time to make up a combination, keeping in mind that a different order is a different combination.

Ordered Combination Formula

To calculate the number of combinations from a group of items when order is important, the following formula is used (Hays 1988, 123):

$$C = \frac{n!}{(n-r)!}$$

Ordered Combination Example

Using the information above, the statistician wishes to determine how many combinations he can come up with using 4 letters (A, B, C, and D) if he selects 3 at a time,

Table 2.3.   Letter Combinations

ABC	ABD	ACB	ACD	ADB	ADC
BAC	BAD	BCA	BCD	BDA	BDC
CAB	CAD	CBA	CBD	CDA	CDB
DAB	DAC	DBA	DBC	DCA	DCB

and a different order represents a different combination. The variable n is equal to 4 since there are 4 letters, and the variable r is equal to 3 since there are 3 letters selected at a time.

$$C = \frac{n!}{(n-r)!} = \frac{4!}{(4-3)!} = \frac{24}{1} = 24$$

The result of 24 means that there are 24 different combinations that 3 letters can be placed in, with a different order representing a different combination, and there are 4 items to select from. The sample space for this result is displayed in Table 2.3.

COMBINATIONS

In some situations, the order of the items is not important. When this is the case, then the statistician uses the combination formula. Using the same steps as with ordered combinations, the statistician determines how many combinations can be made using a lesser number of items than the total available, but this time, a combination of ABC is treated as the same as a combination of BCA, CAB, ACB, BAC, and CBA. The variables for the combination formula are the same as for ordered combinations.

Combination Formula

Because the order of the letter sequences does not matter, the following formula is used to determine the number of sequences (Hays 1988, 125):

$$P = \frac{n!}{r!(n-r)!}$$

Combination Example

Again using the information above, the statistician wishes to determine how many combinations he can come up with using 4 letters (A, B, C, and D) if he selects 3 at a time, but this time the order of the letters is not important. The variable n is equal to 4 since there are 4 letters, and the variable r is equal to 3 since there are 3 letters selected at a time.

$$P = \frac{n!}{r!(n-r)!} = \frac{4!}{3!(4-3)!} = \frac{24}{6} = 4$$

Table 2.4.   Letter Combinations

ABC	ABD	ACD	BCD

The obtained value of 4 means that there are 4 different combinations that 3 letters can be placed in given the fact that the order of the letters is not important. The sample space is displayed in Table 2.4.

Binomial Probabilities

In situations where there are only two possible outcomes for an event, such as a heads/tails or yes/no situation, the distribution is considered to be binomial. In these cases binomial probabilities must be derived because the possible numbers of outcomes are set into the two possible outcomes that can be considered a discrete variable. Flipping a coin a number of times and determining the probability that it will land on heads a specific number of times meets the binomial probability since there are only two possible outcomes, heads and tails.

BINOMIAL PROBABILITY FORMULA

The formula presented below can be used to determine the binomial probability (Hays 1988, 130–32).

$$P = \frac{n!}{r!(n-r)!}(P^r)(1-P)^{n-r}$$

Where n = number of possible outcomes; r = number of desired outcomes; P = probability of one failure.

BINOMIAL PROBABILITY EXAMPLE

A person flips a coin 5 times and it lands on tails 4 of the 5 times. What is the probability of this occurring? If we were to try to use the joint event probability of $P(T \& T \& T \& T \& H) = (1/2) \times (1/2) \times (1/2) \times (1/2) \times (1/2)$, we would always end up with the same probability of 3.13%, no matter what the outcome. In the binomial probability function formula, n is equal to the number of times the coin is flipped, r is the number of times tails comes up, and P is the probability of 1 event; in this case, the probability of obtaining tails after 1 flip is .5. Using the above equation,

$$P = \frac{5!}{4!(5-4)!}(.5^4)(1-.5)^{5-4} = \begin{array}{l}\text{.16, or 16\% chance of obtaining tails 4} \\ \text{times when flipping a coin 5 times}\end{array}$$

Poisson Probability

The Poisson probability function is probably one of the most important to the safety professional. Poisson probabilities are used to determine the probability of an event when the frequency of their occurrence is quite low in comparison to the overall exposure. Many types of accident occurrences can be expected to follow a Poisson distribution, for which a Poisson probability must be calculated.

POISSON PROBABILITY FORMULA

The Poisson probability formula uses an expected number of mishaps based on previous experience (Hays 1988, 144–45).

$$P_X = \frac{e^{-M}M^X}{X!}$$

Where $M = NP$; $E = 2.178$; N = exposure period; P = probability of one mishap; X = number of mishaps in question; M = expected number of mishaps during an exposure period.

POISSON PROBABILITY EXAMPLE

Based on past data, a system was found to have 3 failures after 25,000 hours of operation. Modifications were made to the system that were intended to reduce the number of failures. The system was run for 55,000 hours, during which time it had 2 failures. What was the probability of this happening?

The first step is to solve for M, which is considered the expected number of failures. This is determined by multiplying the number of exposure units (N) by the probability of 1 failure (P). In this example, the exposure under investigation is 55,000 hours, and the probability of 1 failure is 1.2×10^{-4}. During the 55,000 hours, there would be 6.6 failures ($1.2 \times 10^{-4} \times 55,000$) based on previous conditions. The term e is the base of a natural logarithm and has the value 2.718, and the variable X represents the specific number of failures being investigated. In this example, $X = 2$.

$$P_{2\ \text{failures in 55,000 hours}} = \frac{2.718^{-6.6} \times 6.6^2}{2} = \frac{.03, \text{ or 3\% chance of 2 failures in}}{55,000 \text{ hours}}$$

$$M = NP = 55,000(1.2 \times 10^{-4}) = 6.6$$

Chapter Summary

This chapter covered the basic concepts of probability and the various formats that probabilities can take. When determining a probability, the statistician must determine the type of probability that is appropriate. The key words *and* and *or* in a probability statement determine the type of probability being derived and the formulas that must be used in order to do so properly. The word *and* in a probability statement signifies a joint probability; here the individual events are multiplied. The word *or* in a probability statement signifies a compound probability; here the individual events are added together, keeping in mind the importance of the mutual exclusiveness of the events. If both events can occur at the same time, then the events are not mutually exclusive and the probability of the occurrence of both events must be subtracted out.

In conditional event probabilities, a condition or restriction is placed on the sample and then the probability is determined. These are usually determined using a two-step process.

In some instances, the total number of possible events is not readily known nor obtained by counting subjects. The researcher instead may have to determine the number of possible events using permutations, combinations, or ordered combinations. Knowing what constitutes a combination—for example, whether the order of the items is important—will assist the researcher in applying the proper technique. With the total number of items determined, the various forms of probability functions can be used to calculate probabilities.

Lastly, two additional probability formulas were discussed, binomial and Poisson. Binomial probability should be determined when there are only two possible outcomes, such as yes/no or male/female. Poisson probability is used in the area of accident research, where the occurrences of accidents can be considered small compared to the total possible exposure, which is the criterion for use of this probability function.

Chapter Review Exercises

1. A safety manager decided to perform a quality check on a product that was being produced by the company. He randomly selected 15 units from a box of 100 and found 3 to be damaged. What is the probability of a damaged piece of equipment coming off the production line?
2. A system was set up in parallel with two components, A and B. The probability of failure for A is .20 and for B is .10. In order for the system to fail, both must fail. What is the probability of a system failure?
3. A system was set up in series with two components, A and B. In order for the system to fail, only one must fail. The probability of failure for A is .30 and for B is .20. What is the probability of a system failure?
4. A system was found to average a rate of 2 failures per 30,000 hours of use. What is the probability of one failure to the system in the next 40,000 hours?
5. A system is arranged in parallel with four components. If two components have a probability of failure of .007 and the other two have a probability of failure of .003, what is the probability of a system failure if all components have to fail at the same time?
6. There are seven subjects in a study. Three have a disease and four are disease-free. What is the probability of selecting a person with the disease?

7. What is the probability of selecting a club from a deck of cards?
8. You have eight poker chips, six red and two blue. What is the probability of selecting one red chip?
9. A researcher measures a person's IQ. The IQ can be considered:
    a. a form of error
    b. a variable
    c. a case
    d. interval data
10. $(1/6) \times (1/6) =$
    a. 2/6
    b. 2/36
    c. 1/6
    d. 1/36

CHAPTER 3

Distributions

Statistical Distributions and Populations

If a safety manager wishes to investigate a research problem, and the data is collected and a group of raw numbers is obtained, the first step in beginning to make any sense out of the data is to organize the information in a meaningful format. The formatting begins with some type of order to the numbers, followed by grouping of the data. Once organized, the data can be compared to other data that are similarly organized. These organized data are referred to as distributions.

Frequencies

Frequency is the number of times an event occurs. For example, if a safety manager collects and counts the back injury claims for a given year and comes up with 120, then the frequency of back injuries for the year is 120. The simplest method for organizing frequencies is with a frequency distribution, which can be developed using either grouped or ungrouped data.

FREQUENCY DISTRIBUTION EXAMPLE

An investigator gathers data on the severity of 20 vehicle claims for a given year. The raw data collected was as follows:

$75	$80
$150	$1,200
$150	$540
$2,000	$3,000
$4,500	$2,300
$1,200	$100
$150	$2,500
$2,000	$560
$85	$200
$80	$100

To develop a frequency distribution, the investigator takes the values of the claims and places them in order. Then the investigator counts the frequency of occurrences for each value.

Value	Frequency
$75	1
$80	2
$85	1
$100	2
$150	3
$200	1
$540	1
$560	1
$1,200	2
$2,000	2
$2,300	1
$2,500	1
$3,000	1
$4,500	1
Total	20

To develop a frequency distribution, groupings are formed using the values in the table above, ensuring that each group has an equal range. The investigator decided to group the data into ranges of 1,000. The lowest range and highest range are determined by the data. Since the investigator decided to group by thousands, values will fall in the ranges of $0–$4,999. Because the greatest value obtained for a claim is $4,500, it would fall in the range of $4,000–$4,999, and the distribution will end with this. It would not be correct, for example, to include a range of $5,000–$5,999 because there are no obtained values in that range. The frequency distribution for this data is shown in Table 3.1.

Histograms

Once the data is arranged in a frequency distribution, they can be graphically displayed. Methods include histograms and frequency polygons. A histogram is a column chart depicting the data from the frequency distribution. Using the vehicle

Table 3.1.   Frequency Distribution

Range	Frequency
$0–$999	12
$1,000–$1,999	2
$2,000–$2,999	4
$3,000–$3,999	1
$4,000–$4,999	1
Total	20

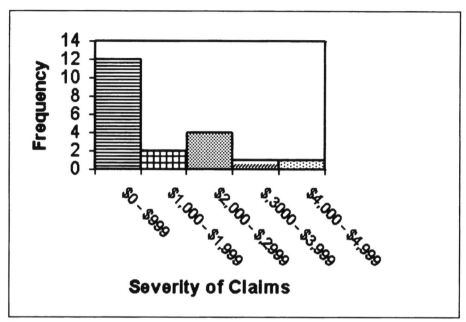

Figure 3.1.   Histogram of Vehicle Claim Data.

claim frequency distribution from above, a histogram is developed, as shown in Figure 3.1.

The histogram consists of two axes with the data displayed inside. The groups for the claims are placed along the horizontal (x) axis, and the frequency of claims is placed along the vertical axis (y), going from 0 to the greatest value obtained for any of the claim value categories.

When developing a histogram, some guidelines should be followed (Freedman et al. 1978, 29–31). The following is a suggested list of guidelines:

- The vertical axis should represent the frequency or percentage of cases in each interval, and the horizontal axis should represent each interval.
- The horizontal axis should be developed using equal intervals.
- There should be no overlaps in the intervals.
- The horizontal and vertical axes should begin at zero.
- Each case in a histogram is represented by an area. This area should be consistent for each case.
- The horizontal and vertical axes should be labeled, as should be the histogram.
- The source for the data in the histogram should be provided either in the title or in a footnote to the histogram.

Frequency Polygons

A frequency polygon is a depiction of the histogram column points. The frequency polygon can be developed using the results from the histogram. The center points at

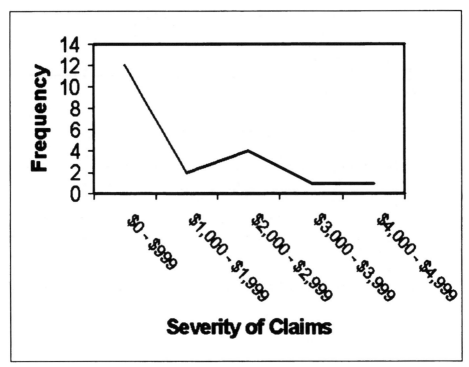

Figure 3.2.   Frequency Polygon for Vehicle Claim Data.

the tops of each of the columns of the histogram are identified and marked with a point. The points are then connected with a line beginning at the 0,0 point and finishing back at the x-axis. An example of the frequency polygon is displayed in Figure 3.2.

Key points for developing a frequency polygon include the following:

- The line for the first data point is connected to the midpoint of the previous interval on the x-axis.
- The line for the last data point is connected to the midpoint of the following interval on the x-axis.

Percentages, Cumulative Percentages, and Percentiles

A percentage is calculated by dividing the frequency of occurrence by the total number of occurrences and then multiplying by 100. In the following example, an ergonomist counted the number of motions performed by a worker during a 1-minute task. The data for the task motions were categorized into groups as shown in Table 3.2.

The percentage of the task motions is then calculated by dividing the frequency of the motions by the total number of motions recorded. For example, the percent-

Table 3.2.   Frequency of Task Motions

Category	Frequency
Above shoulders	12
Between shoulders and waist	15
Between waist and knees	7
Below knees	3
Total	37

age of motions above the shoulders is calculated as (12/37) ¥ 100 for 32.4%. This procedure has been performed for each of the categories in Table 3.1 and is displayed in Table 3.3.

The next step is to calculate the cumulative percentage. In this example, the percentages for each category are added to the sum of the percentages for all of the preceding categories in the list, with the last category summing 100%. Cumulative percentages can be used to summarize categories. In this example, it can easily be determined from the cumulative percentages that 72.9% of the job task motions occur from the waist and above.

Normal Distribution

When large amounts of data are collected on characteristics such as intelligence, the histogram of the data and subsequent frequency polygon can follow a distribution that is bell-shaped. We have identified methods for developing a histogram from raw data and then from the histogram, developing a frequency polygon. The greatest frequency of cases is lumped around the center of the distribution, and as we move away from the center, the frequency of cases steadily decreases in both directions. When this occurs, we are left with a bell-shaped curve for a frequency polygon (see Figure 3.3). While an exact normal distribution is hypothetical in nature, we use this normal distribution curve to compare results obtained in statistics to what could have been obtained in actuality.

In addition to the bell-shaped curve, some common deviations can occur to the curve owing to the distribution of data. Some of the most common types of curves are referred to as positively skewed curves, negatively skewed curves, and bimodal curves (Horvath 1974, 33). A positively skewed curve has the majority of the observations in

Table 3.3.   Cumulative Percentage of Task Motions

Category	Frequency	Percentage	Cumulative Percentage
Above shoulders	12	32.4	32.4
Between shoulders and waist	15	40.5	72.9
Between waist and knees	7	19.0	91.9
Below knees	3	8.1	100.0
Total	37	100.0	

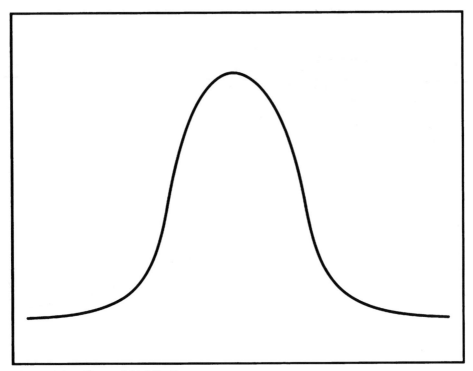

Figure 3.3.   Normal Distribution.

the area toward the lower end of the x-axis, while a negatively skewed curve has the majority of the observations in the upper region of the x-axis. A bimodal curve is one that has two peaks. These curves are depicted in Figures 3.4–3.6.

Binomial Distribution

In Chapter 2, binomial probability distribution was introduced as the correct procedure for determining the probability of the occurrence of events that have two possible outcomes. When an array of probabilities is derived for a series of possible outcomes, a binomial distribution can be developed. The binomial distribution consists of the categories of possible outcomes along the x-axis and the probability of their occurrence along the y-axis.

BINOMIAL DISTRIBUTION EXAMPLE

A safety engineer wanted to develop the binomial distribution depicting the occurrence of failures for a component in a testing procedure. Five components were to be tested at a time, so the engineer developed the binomial distribution for the chances of

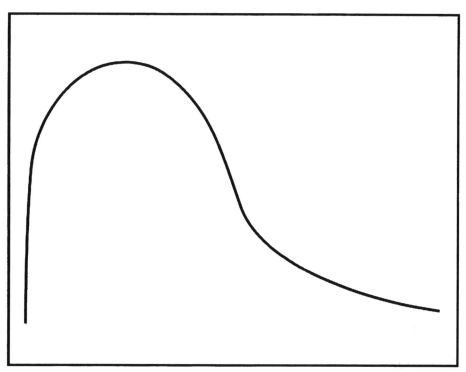

Figure 3.4.   Positively Skewed Curve.

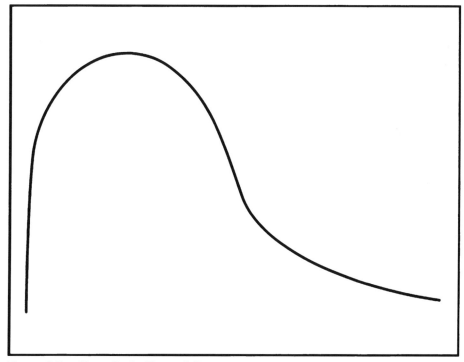

Figure 3.5.   Negatively Skewed Curve.

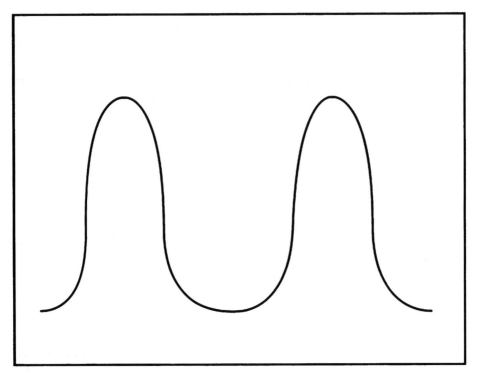

Figure 3.6.   Bimodal Distribution.

having failed components in a group of five. It was determined through prior testing that the probability of failure for one component was 50%.

To determine the probability of failure for 0 failures in 5 components, the following formula was used:

$$P = \frac{n!}{r!(n - r)!}\,(P^r)(1 - P)^{n - r}$$

Where n = number of components; r = number of failures; P = probability of 1 failure.

Probability Results

$$P(0 \text{ Failure}) = \frac{5!}{0!(5 - 0)!}\ .50^0(1 - .50)^{5 - 0} = .03, \text{ or } 3\%$$

$$P(1 \text{ Failure}) = \frac{5!}{1!(5 - 1)!}\ .50^1(1 - .50)^{5 - 1} = .16, \text{ or } 16\%$$

$$P(2 \text{ Failures}) = \frac{5!}{2!(5-2)!} \ .50^2(1-.50)^{5-2} = .31, \text{ or } 31\%$$

$$P(3 \text{ Failures}) = \frac{5!}{3!(5-3)!} \ .50^3(1-.50)^{5-3} = .31, \text{ or } 31\%$$

$$P(4 \text{ Failures}) = \frac{5!}{4!(5-4)!} \ .50^4(1-.50)^{5-4} = .16, \text{ or } 16\%$$

$$P(5 \text{ Failures}) = \frac{5!}{5!(5-5)!} \ .50^5(1-.50)^{5-5} = .03, \text{ or } 3\%$$

The distribution of the results is shown in Table 3.4.

The binomial distribution histogram is shown in steps rather than a smooth curve as is obtained with the normal distribution curve (see Figure 3.7).

t Distribution

In our discussion about the normal distribution curve, the assumptions the data had to meet to be considered normally distributed included the need for data that were measured on a continuous scale (such as age, height, and weight) and collected from a large sample. In some situations, it may not be possible to gather the amounts of data necessary or the data just may not be available. Because of these limitations, we should not assume a normal distribution. Rather we may use the *t* distribution.

The *t* distribution can be used to test hypotheses using a small numbers of cases. For the purposes of this text, and as has been defined by other statisticians, a small number of cases can be considered to be fewer than 25 subjects. The *t* distribution uses the concept of degrees of freedom to establish the shape of the curve and the determination of the critical values for the various statistics that employ the distribution. As the numbers of cases get larger, the distribution more closely resembles the normal distribution's bell-shaped curve (see Figure 3.8).

Table 3.4. Binomial Distribution Results

Failures	Probability	Cumulative Probability
0	0.03	3%
1	0.16	19%
2	0.31	50%
3	0.31	81%
4	0.16	97%
5	0.03	100%

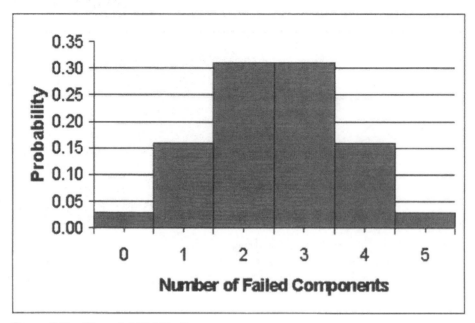

Figure 3.7.   Binomial Distribution.

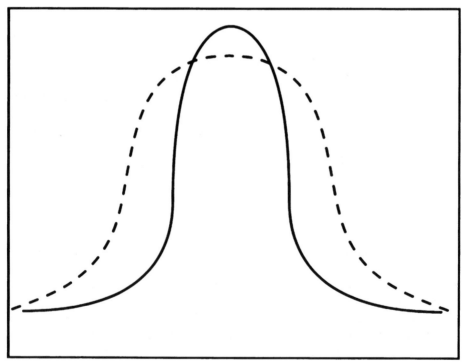

Figure 3.8.   _t_ Distribution.

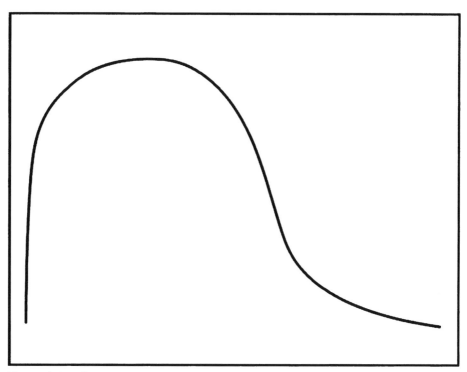

Figure 3.9. Chi-square Distribution.

Chi-square Distribution

The chi-square distribution is used to make inferences about a single population variance. The chi-square is always a squared quantity, so the values will always be positive. The chi-square distribution also utilizes the degrees of freedom, the numbers of which are determined by the statistical test. The shape of the chi-square distribution for approximately 8 degrees of freedom is displayed in Figure 3.9.

F Distribution

The F distribution was derived by the statistician Sir Ronald Fisher. It compares two population variances in the form of a ratio called an F ratio. The F ratio is actually formed by the ratio of two chi-square variables, each divided by its own degree of freedom. Using two independent samples, the ratio between the two variances can be used to calculate the F ratio. The F ratio can be derived and the degrees of freedom calculated for each as $(n - 1)$. An F distribution table is used to determine significance. Like the chi-square distribution, F ratios will be positive numbers because of the use of squared numbers in their calculation. The F distribution also changes shape as the degrees of freedom change.

Chapter Summary

The first step in conducting research is to organize the data in a meaningful way. A fundamental way of doing this is through the development of a frequency distribution. The investigator orders the data in sets from lowest to highest in terms of possible outcomes. For each range of potential outcomes, the frequency of cases is identified and listed. From the frequency distribution, histograms, frequency polygons, and distributions can be identified for the data.

The researcher must know what type of distribution the data take on so he or she can properly choose the statistical tests and make correct decisions about the data. There are five major distributions identified for the data: normal distribution, t distribution, F distribution, chi-square distribution, and binomial distribution.

While the normal distribution, commonly referred to as the "bell-shaped" curve, maintains its hypothetical shape, the other distributions are dependent on the data sets being analyzed. The shape of the curve is dependent on the number of cases, which determines the degrees of freedom for the statistical test. As the degrees of freedom change, the shape of the distribution also changes.

Chapter Review Exercises

1. Describe the process one would follow to set up a frequency distribution.
2. What information would a frequency distribution provide a researcher?
3. What information would a frequency polygon provide?
4. Using the following data set, develop a frequency distribution.

   34, 33, 35, 36, 56, 54, 54, 55, 56, 34, 56

5. Give an example of a data set in which a normal distribution would be assumed.
6. Give an example of a data set in which a t distribution would be assumed.
7. Give an example of a data set in which a binomial distribution would be assumed.
8. Develop a histogram for the following data.

   9, 4, 2, 5, 7, 5, 10, 12, 12, 3, 3, 2, 6, 4, 2

9. A safety manager collected data for a process and found that in a batch of items, there was a 20% chance that a component was defective. The safety manager wishes to know, if he selects 6 components at a time, what the probability of selecting 0, 1, 2, 3, 4, 5, and 6 failed components is in a selection of 6 components.
10. Develop the cumulative frequency distribution for the scenario presented in Exercise 9.

CHAPTER 4

Descriptive Statistics

Data Formats

Data used for statistical research and analysis can be classified into four major categories according to the characteristics of the numbers: categorical, ordinal, interval, and ratio (Horvath 1974, 16–20). It is important to correctly identify the format of the data because the various statistical methods are dependent on it. Researchers can use computers to determine the outcomes for an analysis. Although a computer will provide an answer for a statistical test, it may be meaningless because the data format has violated the assumptions of the statistical procedure.

CATEGORICAL DATA

Categorical or *discrete data* is data that represents categories. Categorical data can be referred to as dichotomous if it has only two categories. When setting up categorical data, the researcher determines the definitions to the various categories and assigns a different number to each. The number signifies nothing more than that category 1 is different from category 2. These data values do not have magnitude, meaning a category numbered 2 is not twice as large as a category 1. An example of categorical data is the gender of a person (male or female), the department that a person works in, etc. When establishing categorical data, the researcher typically provides the categories and asks the respondent to select one, or categories are developed and the researcher assigns placement.

ORDINAL DATA

Ordinal data is rank order data. Ordinal means order, and ordinal data allows the researcher to order the data in some fashion. Examples of ordinal data include any type of ranking exercise, such as requiring the respondent to rank items from 1 to 10. Likert scales are another form of ordinal data. When a person is asked to select a number on a Likert scale, it is possible to arrange the answers into some order from best to worst, highest to lowest, etc. Likert scales are considered a form of continuous data; however, the concept of magnitude does not exist. Magnitude is an ability to make comparisons between the values of a scale. With an ordinal scale, one cannot say that a ranking of 4 is twice as good as a ranking of 2. One can say, however, that the item ranked 1 is ranked above an item ranked 4, assuming one knows that the rankings improve the lower they go.

INTERVAL DATA

Interval data is considered a form of continuous data. Interval data has zero as a place-holder on the scale. An example of a scale that is interval is the Fahrenheit scale. An interval scale does not have magnitude. For example, a researcher has two beakers of water. The water in one is 100°F and in the other is 50°F. While it is correct to say the 100°F water is warmer than the 50°F water, it is not correct to say it is twice as hot. While it may appear to be the case, this comparison would not hold true if one beaker of water were 100°F and the other was 0°F.

RATIO DATA

The last data format to be discussed is ratio data. *Ratio data* is continuous data and the scale does not have zero as a placeholder. The zero on this scale represents absence of that characteristic. Examples of ratio data include height and weight. If an object has a weight of zero then it does not have the characteristic of weight. Ratio data is the only scale in which magnitude between values on the scale exists. If one item weighs 10 lb. and the other 5 lb., then it is correct to say that the first item is twice as heavy as the second.

Strength of the Data Formats

As the data formats move from categorical to ordinal, interval, and finally ratio, their flexibility in terms of the statistical tests one can use also increases. Starting with categorical, this data format provides the least flexibility in terms of statistical testing. Categorical data cannot be recoded into anything, but categorical data and the types of statistics one can use are referred to as nonparametric. As one moves up the scales, ordinal data can be recoded into a categorical data format, but it cannot be recoded into interval or ratio. Interval data can be recoded into ordinal and categorical, and ratio can be recoded into any of the data formats. As one can see, ratio data provides the greatest flexibility for statistical analysis. It can be used with any number of statistical procedures mainly because the researcher can recode the data into any of the other data formats.

Measures of Central Tendency

The first group of descriptive statistics is defined as the measures of central tendency. These statistics describe how closely the data groups together. There are three measures of central tendency. They are the mean, median, and mode (Hays 1988, 155–56).

MEAN

The *mean* is the arithmetic average of a distribution of numbers. The mean is derived by summing the items and dividing by the total number of items in the distribution. For example, an ergonomist collected five stature measurements. The measurements were (in inches) 72, 65, 60, 58, and 54. The average is calculated using the following formula:

$$\overline{x} = \frac{\Sigma x}{n}$$

Mathematically, the following is performed:

$$\overline{X} = \frac{(72 + 65 + 60 + 58 + 54)}{5} = 61.8 \text{ in.}$$

MEDIAN

The *median* is the point at which 50% of the values lie above and 50% lie below. It is based on the number of items, not the actual values per se. For example, if we use the measurements noted earlier, the median would be determined by first arranging the values in order from lowest to highest 54, 58, 60, 65, 72. Because there are 5 numbers, the median is the middle number that the array would balance on if they were on a fulcrum. In this example, the median number is 60 inches.

$$\underline{54 \quad 58 \quad 60 \quad 65 \quad 72}$$
$$\blacktriangle$$

To calculate the median with an even number of items, the researcher must first arrange the numbers from lowest to highest. Using the two middle numbers, the average is computed and becomes the median. An example would be as follows: An investigator collected 6 readings from a pressure valve for a sprinkler system. The readings (in psi) were as follows:

$$45, 37, 46, 37, 43, 39$$

To calculate the median, the investigator first reorders the numbers from lowest to highest:

$$37, 37, 39, 43, 45, 46$$

The middle two points would be 39 and 43. Averaging the two numbers yields 41 [(39 + 43)/2]; thus the median for this distribution is 41.

MODE

The *mode* of a distribution is the most frequently occurring number in the distribution, and is determined by identifying the number that appears most often. Distributions can have one mode, two modes, more than two modes, or no mode at all. Using the data that the safety manager collected from the sprinkler system valve readings, the most frequently occurring number in the distribution is 37, since it appears twice and more often than any other number in the distribution. Thus 37 would be considered the mode of the distribution.

Earlier we examined the normal distribution curve, also known as the bell-shaped curve. On the hypothetical bell-shaped curve, the mean, median, and mode are all the same number and are located at the center of the curve.

Measures of Variability

There are three measures of variability. These measures indicate the spread of the data and are the range, variance, and standard deviation (Hays 1988, 171–76).

RANGE

The *range* of a data set is the difference between the lowest value and the highest value data points. In order to calculate the range, the data must be arranged from lowest to highest. Subtracting the lowest data point value from the highest data point value yields the range. For example, a loss control consultant obtained the frequency of hazards identified at each of six sites visited over the period of a week. The numbers of hazards recorded were as follows:

$$6, 6, 5, 4, 9, 5$$

To determine the range, first the values are placed in order from lowest to highest: 4, 5, 5, 6, 6, 9. The lowest value for the distribution is 4 while the highest is 9. The range is 5 (i.e., 9 – 4).

VARIANCE

The *variance* of a distribution is a measure of how much the individual data points vary from the distribution mean. The variance is the average of the squared deviations from the mean and is calculated using the formula presented in Equation 4.1. A deviation is the difference between the data point and the distribution's mean. When calculating the variance for a sample, the numerator is $n - 1$. For a population, the numerator is n.

Equation 4.1 Variance Formula

$$\sigma^2 = \frac{\Sigma (x - \bar{x})^2}{n - 1}$$

Using the data set above, the first step is to determine the average. Using the formula presented previously, the average is calculated as follows:

$$\bar{x} = \frac{(6 + 6 + 5 + 4 + 9 + 5)}{6} = 5.8$$

Using the mean of 5.8, the differences between each data point and the average is calculated. The mean is then subtracted from each data point to yield the deviation. Table 4.1 depicts this process.

The top term in the formula requires the statistician to sum the squared difference values for all cases. In this example, that total is 14.84 (see the section Variance Calculation). The final step is to divide this sum by the total number of cases, which is represented by n. In this example, there are 6 cases, so $n - 1$ equals 5. The variance for this distribution is therefore 2.97.

Variance Calculation

$$\sigma^2 = \frac{14.84}{5} = 2.97$$

Table 4.1. Variance Example

Data Value	Mean	Deviation Score (Column 1 – Column 2)	Squared Deviation Score ((Column 3)^2)
6	5.8	0.2	0.04
6	5.8	0.2	0.04
5	5.8	−0.8	0.64
4	5.8	−1.8	3.24
9	5.8	3.2	10.24
5	5.8	−0.8	0.64
Total			14.84

STANDARD DEVIATION

Standard deviation is the average difference from the mean for the scores in a distribution. The standard deviation is derived by taking the square root of the variance.

$$\sigma = \sqrt{\sigma^2}$$

In the example above, the standard deviation would be as follows:

$$\sigma = \sqrt{2.97} = 1.72$$

Standard deviations can be used as population markers to determine the expected ranges for scores in a given distribution. One hears statements like "a person scored 3 standard deviations above the population average" or "a value is 2 standard deviations below the mean." The standard deviation can be used to establish these reference points on a distribution. In the previous chapter, we discussed the normal distribution or bell-shaped curve. By examining the curve more closely, it is possible to determine the percentage of the population between various points on the curve.

By definition, in a bell-shaped curve we expect to find approximately 68% of the population between +1 and −1 standard deviations, approximately 95% of the population between +2 and −2 standard deviations, and approximately 99% of the population between +3 and −3 standard deviations. It is also known that the curve comprises 100% of the population, and one would expect to find 50% of the population above the median and 50% below the median.

INTERQUARTILE RANGE

A measure associated with the range is the *interquartile range* (Witte and Witte 1997, 75–76). This range is the middle 50% of all observations in the distribution and is the distance between the upper end of the first quartile and the upper end of the third quartile. The first quartile is the point where 25% of the population lies below, and the third quartile is the point where 25% of the population lies above. The interquartile range is the difference between these two points.

To determine the quartiles, order the number of observations from lowest to highest. Count the number of observations, add one to that number and divide by four. If necessary, round the result to the nearest whole number. This value gives the number of observations to move up to from the low end of the distribution and the number of observations to move down to from the upper end of the distribution.

Interquartile Range Sample Problem

An investigator collected data from a set of 15 observations and wishes to calculate the interquartile range. The cases are as follows:

12, 34, 33, 22, 40, 18, 21, 14, 35, 38, 29, 28, 26, 19, 36

The first step is to rearrange the data from lowest to highest:

12, 14, 18, 19, 21, 22, 26, 28, 29, 33, 34, 35, 36, 38, 40

In this example, the upper and lower quartiles are calculated by adding the number of observations, adding 1, and then dividing by 4 as follows:

$$(15 + 1)/4 = 4$$

From the lower end of the distribution (the left), one counts in four observations to a case score of 19. This is the lower quartile. For the upper quartile (the right), one counts down four observations from the highest observation to 35. This is the upper quartile. The interquartile range is the difference between the two points $(35 - 19) = 16$.

z Scores

The standard deviation can also be used to convert raw scores into z scores. A z score can be used to identify the location of a raw score on the normal distribution curve. The z scores can then be used with a z table to determine percentages of populations and probabilities associated with the normal distribution.

Z SCORE FORMULA

To convert a raw score to a z score, the following formula is used (Kuzma 1992, 82):

$$z = \frac{x - \bar{x}}{\sigma}$$

Z SCORE SAMPLE PROBLEM

An investigator obtained the following set of raw data:

23	44
21	26
34	67
45	66
54	42
45	22
67	47
34	55

The investigator would like to know what the z score is for a raw score of 46. To answer this question, the investigator must first calculate the mean and the standard deviation for the distribution. The calculated mean for the distribution is 43.3, while the standard deviation is 15.8. The z score is

$$z = \frac{46.0 - 43.3}{15.8} = .17$$

To interpret this z score, one could determine the percentage of the population that lies above or below .17 on the normal distribution curve.

Z SCORES AND PERCENTAGES OF THE POPULATION

Using a z table, one can determine the percentages of a population expected to score above and below the obtained z score. All z scores to the right of the mean are positive, while all z scores to the left of the mean are negative. The table values range from +3.49 to −3.49. The first step in reading the z table is to locate the z score on the table. (A z table appears in Appendix A.) The first column of the cumulative distribution for the standard normal random number table corresponds to the first two digits of the z score, while the remaining columns correspond to the two digits following the decimal

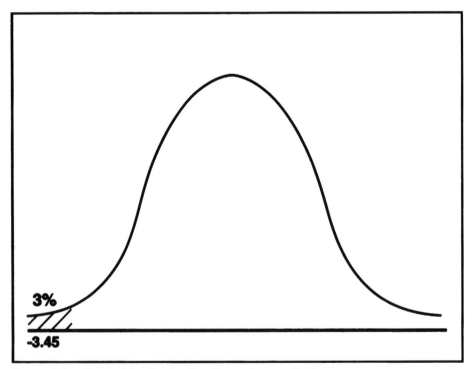

Figure 4.1. Critical Region for the Curve for z = −3.45.

place. The value in the table corresponds to the percentage of the area of the curve that lies between the z score in question and the remaining area of the curve that lies to the left of the z score. For example, to locate a z score of –3.45, go to the first column and locate –3.4 since these numbers correspond to the first two digits of the number. The digit located in the second decimal place is a 5, so go across to the column labeled .05. The number in the table that is in row –3.4 and column .05 is .0003. Multiplying this number by 100 indicates that .03% of the population is expected to lie between the z score of –3.45 and the tail end of the curve (see Figure 4.1).

In our previous example, we obtained a z score of .22. Following the steps above, the investigator initially goes to the first column and finds the row labeled 0.2. Next, the investigator goes to the column labeled .02 and finds the number .5871. This indicates that 58.71% of the population is expected to lie between the z score and the tail end of the curve (see Figure 4.2).

It is also possible to determine the percentages of the population expected to lie between two known points on the curve. There are sets of points that are significant in terms of statistical importance. Many times researchers want to know the points that 95% and 99% of the population lie between, above, or below. When decisions are made regarding inferential statistics, these critical levels are often used. To determine the points between which 95% of the population lies, an assumption that the curve equals 100% is made. When the population is equally distributed to both sides of the curve, there should be 2.5% of the population above and 2.5% below. One would find

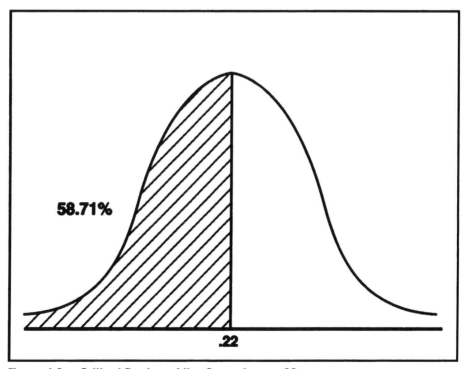

Figure 4.2.   Critical Region of the Curve for z = .22

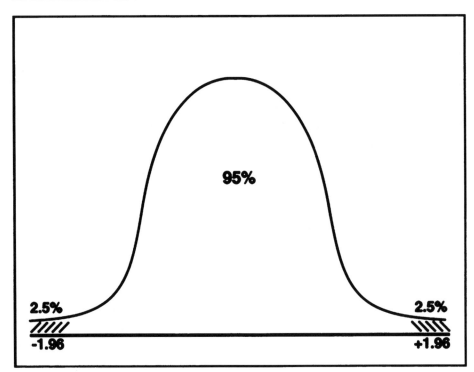

Figure 4.3.   Critical Region of the Curve (95%).

97.5% of the population above the one point and 2.5% above the upper point. Using the table, the z score at which 97.5% of the population lies above is 1.96. This is found in the 1.9 row of the first column and the .06 column. For the other point in which 2.5% of the population lies above, the −1.9 row and the .06 column indicate that 2.5% should lie above this point. Because the curve is a mirror image with the mean serving as the middle point, one would expect to find the same numbers, with the lower number being negative and the upper number being positive (see Figure 4.3).

Using this same process, the upper and lower bounds for 99% of the population can be found. The points on the table yield values of −2.58 and +2.58. This gives 99% of the population in the center and .5% at each end (see Figure 4.4).

In other situations, the researcher may wish to identify the percentage of the population that lies above or below a certain z score. Using the steps above, a z score of −1.65 would identify 95% of the population below this point and 5% above. A z score of +1.65 would identify 5% of the population below this point and 95% above. A z score of −2.33 would identify 99% of the population below this point and 1% above, and a z score of 2.33 would identify 99% of the population above this point and 1% below.

Statistical tests that test for greater-than and less-than situations are considered one tailed. In a one-tailed test, the critical region of the curve is at either one end or the other. Again, if the result of the statistical test lands in the shaded region of the curve, then it is considered to be significant. Figure 4.5 indicates the critical regions of the curves for one-tailed tests.

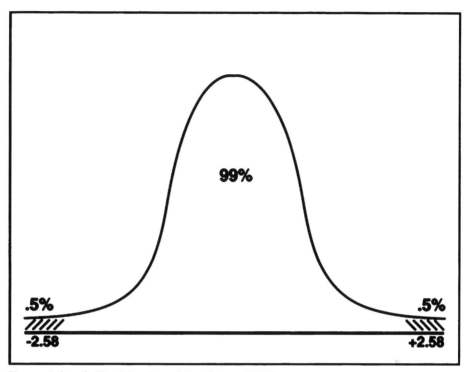

Figure 4.4.   Critical Region of the Curve (99%).

Confidence Intervals for Means

A confidence interval provides a range within which the mean for a distribution can be expected to fall with a certain degree of probability (Kuzma 1992, 105–7). The two most common confidence intervals are the 95% confidence interval ($CI_{95\%}$) and the 99% confidence interval ($CI_{99\%}$). For each confidence interval, there is a lower limit and an upper limit. The 95% confidence interval, for example, can be interpreted as the "true" mean for a distribution that has a 95% probability of falling between the upper and lower limits of the confidence interval. Although a mean was calculated, due to potential statistical biases, the true mean could actually vary in the range of the confidence interval.

95% CONFIDENCE INTERVALS

A researcher wishes to calculate the 95% Confidence Interval ($CI_{95\%}$) for the following data set:

67, 45, 67, 56, 69, 89, 90 87, 88

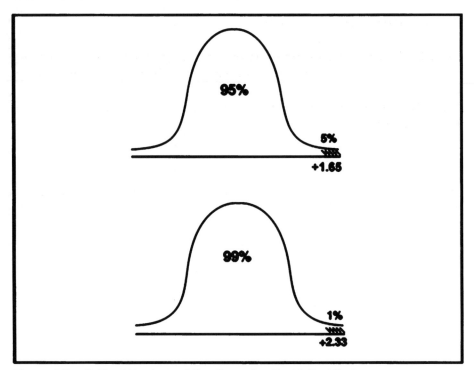

Figure 4.5.   Critical Regions of the Curve for One-tailed Tests

The first step is to determine the mean where the distribution was determined to be 73.1 and the standard deviation was 16.3. The formula for calculating the $CI_{95\%}$ is presented as follows:

$$CI_{95\%} = X \text{ +/- } (1.96)(\sigma / \sqrt{N})$$

If you recall, the 1.96 is from the normal distribution that identifies the point at which 2.5% of the curve remains above. First, to calculate the upper limit, the formula yields:

$$CI_{95\%} = 73.1 + (1.96)(16.3/3) = 83.8$$

The lower limit is calculated using the same formula but substituting the +1.96 with −1.96, which is the point on a normal distribution at which 2.5% of the curve lies below.

$$CI_{95\%} = 73.1 - (1.96)(16.3/3) = 62.5$$

For this distribution, the $CI_{95\%}$ is 62.5 and 83.8. In statistical notation, it is written as

$$CI_{95\%}(62.5, 83.8).$$

99% CONFIDENCE INTERVALS

The $CI_{99\%}$ is calculated in the same manner as the $CI_{95\%}$; however, the 1.96 is replaced with 2.58 in the formula. The value 2.58 corresponds to the normal distribution curve. The +2.58 is the point on the curve at which 0.5% of the curve lies above this point and −2.58 is the point below which 0.5% of the curve lies. Therefore, 99% of the curve lies between the two.

$$CI_{99\%} = X +/- (2.58)(\sigma / \sqrt{N})$$

Using the data provided in the $CI_{95\%}$ example, the researcher calculates the $CI_{95\%}$ as follows:

Upper Limit

$$CI_{99\%} = 73.1 + (2.58)(16.3 / 3) = 87.1$$

Lower Limit

$$CI_{99\%} = 73.1 - (2.58)(16.3 / 3) = 59.1$$

INTERPRETING CONFIDENCE INTERVALS

The confidence interval is interpreted as the interval within which we have an assured degree of probability the true mean will lie. Using the example from above, the $CI_{99\%}$ is interpreted as follows:

In this distribution, we obtained a mean of 73.1. We have a 99% probability that the true mean for this distribution lies somewhere between 59.1 and 87.1. There is only a 1% chance that the mean will lie outside of this range.

Chapter Summary

Descriptive statistics, such as frequencies, percentages, and cumulative percentages, are used to describe a population. Measures of central tendency—the mean, median, and mode—provide an indication of how closely related the data are, while the variance, standard deviation, and range give an indication as to how varied the data are.

With z scores, researchers can make some determinations about the data in a study compared to a normal population. The scores identify the placement of a data point on the normal distribution. From this point on the normal distribution, a researcher can make some determination about the percentages of a population expected to score above or below a point, or between two points.

A confidence interval is a method of determining, with a certain degree of probability, the range within which a mean for a population is expected to fall. Because statistics cannot determine exact values for a sample, the confidence interval gives the researcher a degree of certainty that a mean will fall within an upper point and a lower point. The two most common confidence intervals for means are the 95% and the 99%.

Chapter Review Exercises

Use the following data set to complete Exercises 1–3: (3, 5, 8, 10, 4, 6, 3, 16, 19, 12)

1. What is the mean?
2. What is the standard deviation?
3. What percentage of the population is expected to score above 9?
4. What is the mean of the following distribution?

$$3, 6, 8, 12, 14, 19, 17, 3, 6, 2$$

5. What percentage of the population is expected to score below 5?
6. Within which two scores is 95% of the population expected to score?
7. What is the 99% confidence interval for this data?
8. What percentage of the population is expected to obtain a z score of at least 1.56?
9. How many possible combinations can you obtain with seven items? (A different order signifies a different combination.)
10. Fred has 10 cars, each of a different color. If he decided to select 3 at a time, how many combinations could he come up with? (Order is not important.)
11. How many combinations can he have with different orders?
12. Calculate the variance of the following data set.

$$2, 13, 17, 15, 19, 23, 4, 6, 7, 8$$

13. Calculate the standard deviation of this data set.
14. What is the range of this data set?
15. A manufacturer of computer chips checks for faulty chips as they come off the production line. In a typical workshift, for every 10,000 chips produced, there are 4 damaged chips identified. A salesperson sold the company a new piece of equipment that he claimed would produce a better-quality chip with fewer defects. After allowing the machine to operate for 3 days, 125,000 chips were produced and 43 defects were identified. Does the new machine produce significantly fewer defective chips than the old one?

CHAPTER 5

Statistical Tests

Statistical Hypotheses

Statistical tests are designed to test a hypothesis. A hypothesis is a statement concerning the belief the researcher has about a particular situation. Each statistical test or procedure has a specific hypothesis that can be confirmed. There are two forms of hypotheses that the researcher must generate in order to properly conduct a test. The null hypothesis is represented by the term H_0, while the alternative hypothesis is represented by the term H_1.

Null and alternative hypotheses can take on a variety of forms. For example, if an investigator wishes to show whether the average test scores for a group of males is significantly different from those for a group of females, the investigator would construct a null hypothesis stating that the average test scores for males is equal to the average test scores for females. The alternative hypothesis would be that the average test scores for males is different from (not equal to) the average test scores for females.

The null and alternative hypotheses would be written as:

$$H_0: \overline{X} \text{ males} = \overline{X} \text{ females}$$
$$H_i: \overline{X} \text{ males} \neq \overline{X} \text{ females}$$

Null and alternative hypotheses can also be tested to determine if one group has a value that is significantly greater or less than an expected value. If, for example, the investigator wishes to show whether the average test scores for males is greater than those for females, the null and alternative hypothesis would be as follows:

$$H_0: \overline{X} \text{ males} \leq \overline{X} \text{ females}$$
$$H_i: \overline{X} \text{ males} > \overline{X} \text{ females}$$

It is the alternative hypothesis that states what the investigator believes the situation to be or what the investigator hopes to prove statistically to be the case. It is the hypothesis being tested that is also used to distinguish between one-tailed and two-tailed tests. When an investigator tests for significant differences between groups, the test is considered a two-tailed test. Significance levels for two-tailed tests use both the upper and lower ends of the curve. If the result of the statistical test lands in the shaded regions of the curve, then it is considered to be significant. Statistical tests that test for greater-than and less-than situations are considered one-tailed. In a one-tailed test, the critical region of the curve is at either one end or the other. Again, if the result of the statistical test lands in the shaded region of the curve, then it is considered to be significant.

It is to be kept in mind that the examples presented here use means with two groups. There are numerous types of hypotheses that can be formulated and tested. One can test hypotheses using means, frequencies, and correlation coefficients, to name a few. One can test one group against another group, a group against a known value, or multiple groups against each other. The types of hypotheses that can be tested depend on the statistical test that is being used and the type of data that have been collected. For each of the various statistical tests presented in this book, the hypotheses that can be tested, the type of data required, and other assumptions of the tests and procedures are discussed.

When hypothesis testing, the investigator can either reject or accept the null hypothesis based on the results of the statistical test. When a statistical test is run, the results will indicate whether the test meets or exceeds a level determined to be significant. If the results are significant, the investigator rejects the null hypothesis and accepts the alternative as being true. If the statistical test indicates that the test is not significant, then the investigator accepts the null hypothesis.

Inferential Statistical Testing

When the results of a statistical test are used to generalize results from a sample to a population, we refer to the statistics as inferential. For example, if a person wishes to determine how a particular population will vote in an election, they could go and ask every registered voter. This would be very expensive and time consuming to attempt, and would probably be impossible to do. Rather, the researcher could select a sample of people that is representative of the population, ask them how they would vote, and, based on the sample results, determine with a degree of certainty how the entire population would have responded had everyone been asked. Inferential statistics allows us to make this assumption about sample results and infer them to the population. We should keep in mind that there will be some error in the obtained results compared to those obtained if everyone were sampled. However, if the sample is properly selected, the potential for error can be reduced to a level that is quite small.

Type I and Type II Errors

There are two major types of error a researcher can make when using inferential statistics and hypothesis testing. They are referred to as Type I and Type II errors.

A Type I error occurs when the statistical tests incorrectly indicate to the researcher that the null hypothesis is false; as a result, the researcher rejects the null hypothesis and accepts the alternative. An example of a Type I error would be when a statistical test indicates that a drug cures a person from a certain disease when in fact it really does not. Because of the statistical test, the researcher incorrectly rejects the null hypothesis and accepts the alternative hypothesis.

A Type II error occurs when the researcher incorrectly accepts the null hypothesis when it is false. The statistician collects the data and performs the statistical test. In the Type II error, the results of the statistical test are not significant, thereby leading the researcher to accept the null hypothesis and conclude that the results are not significant. In reality, however, the null hypothesis should have been rejected and a conclusion reached that there is significance in the findings. Using the drug experiment as an example, the researcher would conclude that the drug is not effective when in reality it is. When this type of error is made, significant findings go unnoticed.

α Levels

When using inferential statistics, the researcher tries to control the probability of making these errors in reaching conclusions about the findings. The probability of committing a Type I error is referred to as the α level (α). The α level is determined by the researcher of the study and can vary from study to study and from test to test. The α level can be considered as the probability of rejecting the null hypothesis when in fact it is true.

Statistical Power of a Test

Related to a Type I and Type II error is the statistical power of a test. Statistical power is defined as the probability of being able to correctly determine if a null hypothesis is truly false. Otherwise stated, it is how accurate a statistical test is in identifying significance when it truly exists. The power of a test is represented by $(1 - \beta)$ with β representing the probability of committing a Type II error. The probability of not correctly identifying significance when it exists is the probability of a Type II error (β). A summary of the relationships between Type I errors, Type II errors, power levels, and α levels is displayed in Table 5.1 (Hays 1988, 261).

Table 5.1. Type I and Type II Errors

Decision Made	Null Hypothesis Is False	Null Hypothesis Is True
Reject null hypothesis	Correct decision $(1 - \beta)$	Incorrect decision, Type I error (α)
Accept null hypothesis	Incorrect decision, Type II error (β)	Correct decision $(1 - \alpha)$

Inferential Statistics Test Procedure

Performing an inferential statistical test can be best accomplished using the following seven-step process:

1. Developing a statistical hypothesis
2. Choosing the appropriate statistical test or procedure
3. Determining the statistical distribution
4. Determining significance levels
5. Formulating a decision rule
6. Running the statistical test
7. Formulating a conclusion and making a decision

1. DEVELOPING A STATISTICAL HYPOTHESIS

The researcher must establish the null hypothesis and the alternative hypothesis. The hypotheses play the most crucial role in statistical testing. The hypotheses are used to determine the format in which the data must be collected, the nature of the distribution that the data will follow, the statistical test that must be used to test the hypothesis, and the critical regions of the curve that will be used.

2. CHOOSING THE APPROPRIATE STATISTICAL TEST OR PROCEDURE

Once the hypotheses are developed, the statistical test that must be used to test them is fairly easy to select. Statistical tests and procedures for the most part test a limited number of hypotheses. With the test or procedure identified, the researcher must identify the statistical assumptions for that particular test. Statistical assumptions are the criteria that one must meet in order to use the statistical test appropriately and ensure that the obtained results are valid. As already discussed, the assumptions include the type of data being analyzed and the hypotheses being tested. Additional hypotheses include randomness of the data being used and minimum numbers of cases in the study, to name a few. Violating assumptions of the statistical test can result in incorrect conclusions.

3. DETERMINING THE STATISTICAL DISTRIBUTION

The statistical distribution of the data is mostly determined by the format of the data and the assumptions of the statistical tests that will be used on the data. Distributions can include the normal distribution, t distribution, and chi-square, to name a few. Statistical tests and procedures are performed with a specific distribution in use.

4. DETERMINING SIGNIFICANCE LEVELS

Significance levels are determined using the distribution, α level, and whether it is a one-tailed test or two-tailed test. The significance levels identify the areas of the distribution in which an obtained test or procedure must fall to be considered significant. As discussed earlier, the researcher determines the α level. With the α level and knowing if the test is one tailed or two tailed from the hypothesis being tested, the significance levels or cutoff scores can be determined.

5. FORMULATING A DECISION RULE

The decision rule is a statement developed by the researcher that describes at which point the null hypothesis is to be rejected and the alternative accepted. When establishing rejection rules, significance of a test or procedure is met when the obtained test procedure value is greater than the identified cutoff score. An example of a decision rule would be as follows:

The researcher will reject the null hypothesis and accept the alternative hypothesis if the obtained z score is greater than the cutoff score.

6. RUNNING THE TEST

With all of the previous steps completed, the researcher can perform the statistical test. This step is a matter of calculating the result.

7. FORMULATING A CONCLUSION AND MAKING A DECISION

The final step in this inferential statistical process is the formulation of a decision based on the results of the statistical test. If the statistical test is significant, then the researcher rejects the null hypothesis and accepts the alternative. The probability of making an incorrect decision based on the results when doing so is equal to the α level. On the other hand, if the test is not significant, the researcher accepts the null hypothesis and concludes that the results are not significant.

Chapter Summary

Statistical testing allows the researcher to make inferences about the data from a sample to a larger population. To be able to take this step, the researcher needs to obtain results from a sample, and with a degree of certainty infer the results to the population without actually having to survey all members of the population.

Statistical testing begins with the formulation of a null and alternative hypothesis. Both must be properly stated in order to correctly select the statistical procedure that tests that type of hypothesis. The next step in hypothesis testing is to select an α level. The α level is the probability of committing a Type I error or rejecting the null hypothesis when the null hypothesis is false. With the α level selected, the researcher then develops a decision rule, performs the test, and compares the results to the critical value. With the test completed, the researcher can make a decision based on the results. A seven-step process, which will be used throughout the remainder of this book, is presented as the framework for conducting statistical tests.

Chapter Review Exercises

1. Develop null and alternative hypotheses for the following situation: A safety manager wishes to know if there are significantly more accidents in department A than in department B.
2. Develop null and alternative hypotheses for the following situation: An ergonomist wishes to determine if there is a significant difference between the average number of repetitive motion injuries for Plant A and Plant B.
3. Develop null and alternative hypotheses for the following situation: A safety trainer wishes to know if the average test scores for Group A are significantly lower than those for Group B.
4. Describe the differences between a Type I error and a Type II error.
5. What is the α level used for?
6. Describe the seven steps required to perform a statistical test.
7. What does β represent?
8. What is the difference between a one-tailed test and a two-tailed test?
9. Give an example of situation that would be tested as a one-tailed test.
10. Give an example of a Type I error.
11. Give an example of a situation that would be tested as a two-tailed test.
12. What critical value on the normal distribution would give the researcher 99% above the point and 1% below?
13. What critical value on the normal distribution would give the researcher 95% below the point and 5% above?

CHAPTER 6

Inferential Statistics for Means

In this chapter, inferential test statistics that test various hypotheses about means will be covered. For each test, the steps for inferential testing will be presented, as well as sample applications for the test statistics and procedures.

z Tests

The z test can be used to test hypotheses involving two means. The hypotheses can test whether a sample mean is significantly greater than, less than, or different from a given population mean.

TEST ASSUMPTIONS

The assumptions that must be met to use the z test include the following (Witte and Witte 1997, 222):

1. The number of subjects in the sample is greater than 25.
2. The distribution for the data on which the mean was calculated should be considered to follow a normal distribution.
3. The standard deviation for the population is known.

HYPOTHESIS CONSTRUCTION

There are varieties of hypotheses that can be tested using the z test. A summary of the hypotheses is displayed below:

1. Null Hypothesis: The sample mean is less than or equal to the population mean.
   Alternative Hypothesis: The sample mean is greater than the population mean.

2. Null Hypothesis: The sample mean is greater than or equal to the population mean.
   Alternative Hypothesis: The sample mean is less than the population mean.
3. Null Hypothesis: The sample mean is equal to the population mean.
   Alternative Hypothesis: The sample mean is not equal to the population mean.

DETERMINE SIGNIFICANCE LEVELS

For each hypothesis tested, a critical score or cutoff region must be identified. This is done using both the hypothesis and the α level. For example, in hypothesis set 1, since a greater-than sign appears in the alternative hypothesis, a one-tailed test is used and the critical region of the curve only appears at one end of the curve (Witte and Witte 1997, 237–40). In this case, the critical region is at the upper end of the curve. In Chapter 4, the critical regions of the curve were identified as the point in which 95% of the curve lies below and 5% lies above in a one-tailed test with an α level of .05.

USING A Z TABLE

Rather than having to calculate the critical values each time one wishes to conduct a z test, the critical values can be obtained from the z table (see Appendix A). This table provides the area of the curve that falls between a z score on the curve and the end of the curve. In this example, we have a one-tailed test and we are looking for the point on the curve at which 95% lies below the point and 5% lies above it. On the z table, the first column represents the first two digits of the z score. The first row going across represents the digit that is located two places to the right of the decimal point in the z score. The values in the table represent the percentage of the population expected to fall from the z score value to the remaining right of the curve.

If we look at the first column and go down to the number "1.6," then go to the column ".05," we see that the value that is at the intersection of the row and column is ".9505." This represents approximately 95% from the value to the left of the table and 5% remaining in the upper area of the table.

If one were looking for the critical values for a two-tailed test, one would have to find the negative z score first on the table. For example, assume an investigator is conducting a two-tailed test with an α level of .05. She must find the critical scores at which 2.5 lies below and 2.5 lies above. Since the table represents the percentage of the population from the z score to the left of that point, the investigator must find the negative z score that accounts for 2.5% and the positive z score that represents 97.5%. Going through the values on the table, the exact percentage of .0250 is found in row –1.9 and column .06, for a z score of –1.96. Continuing through the table, the value .9750 is found at the intersection of row 1.9, and column .06 for a z score of 1.96. Thus, 95% of the population can be found between the z scores of –1.96 and 1.96.

It should be kept in mind that the table has values for positive and negative z scores and that the percentages are different for each. It is also important to note that not all z tables are arranged in the same manner. The investigator must be aware of how the table is arranged and what the table values represent.

FORMULATE A DECISION RULE

The decision rule establishes the point at which the null hypothesis will be accepted or rejected. If the null is rejected, then the alternative is accepted. For the one-tailed test, the decision rule would be to reject the null hypothesis and accept the alternative hypothesis if the obtained z score from the statistical test is greater than the critical score.

Z TEST FORMULA

The formula for calculating the z test is as follows (Witte and Witte 1997, 222):

$$z = \frac{\overline{X}_a - \overline{X}_b}{\sqrt{\dfrac{\sigma_a^2}{n_a} + \dfrac{\sigma_b^2}{n_b}}}$$

Where:

$\overline{x}$ Mean for the group
σ^2 Variance for the group
n   Number of subjects in the group

CONCLUSIONS

The conclusions are reached by comparing the obtained z score to the cutoff score. If the obtained z score is greater than the cutoff score, then the null hypothesis is rejected and the alternative is accepted. The probability of incorrectly rejecting the null hypothesis (Type I Error) because of the results is equal to the α level.

EXAMPLE Z TEST PROBLEM

An industrial hygienist collected readings from a CO meter for a process that was running in the plant. The hygienist collected 30 samples over a two-day period. He wanted to determine if the average CO readings for the two-day period were significantly different from the manufacturer's published average for the system. The manufacturer indicates that the process should have an average reading of 35 ppm, with a variance of 55 ppm. These values were based on a sample of 40 readings. The data were collected and analyzed as follows:

Assumptions: The data meet the assumptions for the z test because

1. It can be assumed that the data meet the normal distribution because CO readings are measured on a ratio scale.
2. There is a sufficient number of cases ($N > 25$).

3. The population mean and standard deviation are known.
4. The hypothesis being tested consists of comparing two means.

Hypothesis: The industrial hygienist wishes to determine if the obtained average is significantly different from the manufacturer's obtained average. The null and alternative hypotheses are as follows:

Null Hypothesis: The sample mean is equal to the population mean of 35 ppm.
Alternative Hypothesis: The sample mean is not equal to the population mean of 35 ppm.

Decision Rule: The industrial hygienist selected an α level of .05; therefore, since a two-tailed test is being conducted, he will reject the null hypothesis and accept the alternative if the obtained z is greater than ± 1.96.
     The ppm readings the industrial hygienist obtained were as follows:

23	21	33	22	26
23	15	32	21	35
24	19	21	23	44
44	37	14	33	37
34	29	30	30	21
23	30	35	25	18

To calculate z, the industrial hygienist must determine the variance and the average ppm reading. Using the formulas provided in Chapter 4, the variance was determined to be 61.9 and the mean 27.4.

$$z = \frac{27.4 - 35.0}{\sqrt{\dfrac{61.9}{30} + \dfrac{55.0}{40}}} = -4.11$$

Conclusions: The obtained z score of -4.11 is greater than the critical score of -1.96 and thus would fall into the shaded area of the curve. Therefore, the industrial hygienist would reject the null hypothesis and accept the alternative hypothesis. He would conclude that the mean CO readings between the obtained plant readings and the manufacturer's readings are significantly different.

t Tests

As with a z test, the t test can be used to test hypotheses involving two means. The major difference between the two tests is in the number of cases involved. t tests are used when the number of cases does not meet the minimum of 30. The t statistic is also used to test the hypothesis that a sample comes from a population with a known mean but an unknown standard deviation.

TEST ASSUMPTIONS

The assumptions that must be met to use the t test include the following (Horvath 1974, 155):

1. The number of subjects in the sample is less than 30.
2. The data are considered to be continuous.
3. The standard deviation for the population mean is unknown.

HYPOTHESIS CONSTRUCTION

There are varieties of hypotheses that can be tested using the t test. Following is a summary of the hypotheses.

1. Null Hypothesis: The sample mean is less than or equal to the population mean.
   Alternative Hypothesis: The sample mean is greater than the population mean.
2. Null Hypothesis: The sample mean is greater than or equal to the population mean.
   Alternative Hypothesis: The sample mean is less than the population mean.
3. Null Hypothesis: The sample mean is equal to the population mean.
   Alternative Hypothesis: The sample mean is not equal to the population mean.

DETERMINE SIGNIFICANCE LEVELS

For each hypothesis tested, a critical score or cutoff region must be identified. This is done by using both the hypothesis and the α level. For example, in hypothesis set 1, since a greater-than sign appears in the alternative hypothesis, a one-tailed test is used, and therefore the critical region of the curve only appears at one end of the curve. In this case, it is at the upper end of the curve. In Chapter 5, the critical regions of the curve were identified as the point where 95% of the curve lies below it and 5% lies above it in a one-tailed test with an α level of .05. For a two-tailed test, 2.5% lies above the upper critical value and 2.5% lies below the lower critical value.

To determine the critical values for the t test, one must calculate the degrees of freedom for the test and use the t table for the appropriate α level. (A t table is presented in Appendix B.) The first column of the table represents the degrees of freedom, while each row represents the α level for a one-tailed test. In an example, an investigator wanted to determine the critical value for a one-tailed t test for a study that has 10 degrees of freedom and an α level of .05. Going down the first column to 10 and across to the column marked .05, the critical value of 1.8125 is present. This represents the critical value for the test. If the obtained t score is greater than this value, then the null hypothesis is rejected and the alternative is accepted.

To identify the critical t value for a two-tailed test, one needs to divide the two-tailed α level by two and read the critical value in that column. For example, the investigator wishes to determine the critical value for a t test with 15 degrees of freedom, a two-tailed test, and an α level of .05. To do this, go down the first column to 15 and across to the .025 column (.05/2). The critical value that intersects this row and column is 2.1314. As is the case with z tables, t tables vary in format, so the investigator must know how the table is arranged.

FORMULATE A DECISION RULE

The decision rule establishes the point at which the null hypothesis will be accepted or rejected. If the null is rejected, then the alternative is accepted. For the one-tailed test, the decision rule would be to reject the null hypothesis and accept the alternative hypothesis if the obtained t score from the statistical test is greater than the critical score.

T TEST FORMULA FOR A SINGLE MEAN

To test the hypothesis that a sample comes from a population with a known mean but an unknown standard deviation, a t statistic is used.

$$t = \frac{x - \bar{x}}{s/\sqrt{n}}$$

Where:

$\bar{x}$ population mean
x sample mean
s sample standard deviation
n number of cases in sample

The significance level is determined using $(n - 1)$ degrees of freedom. The obtained t statistic is compared to the significance level and the appropriate decision is made.

T TEST FORMULA FOR INDEPENDENT GROUPS

The formula for calculating the t test is as follows (Kuzma 1992, 110):

$$t = \frac{\bar{X}_a - \bar{X}_b}{Sp\sqrt{\frac{1}{n_a} + \frac{1}{n_b}}}$$

$$Sp = \sqrt{\frac{S_a^2(n_a-1) + S_b^2(n_b-1)}{n_a + n_b - 2}}$$

$$df = n_a + n_b - 2$$

Where:

$\overline{X_a}$	Mean for group a
$\overline{X_b}$	Mean for group b
S_a^2	Variance for the group a
S_b^2	Variance for the group b
n	Number of subjects in the group
Sp	Pooled standard deviation
df	Degrees of freedom

CONCLUSIONS

The conclusions are reached by comparing the obtained t score to the cutoff score. If the obtained t score is greater than the cutoff score, then the null hypothesis is rejected and the alternative is accepted. The probability of incorrectly rejecting the null hypothesis (Type I Error) because of the results is equal to the α level.

EXAMPLE T TEST PROBLEM

A safety manager wants to determine if there is a significant difference in her plant's average loss per vehicle accident compared to the company average. The safety manager has 15 vehicle accidents in her sample. She wants to compare her average to the company average of $3,200 with a standard deviation of $1,600 based on 24 cases.

Assumptions: The data meet the assumptions for the t test because

1. It can be assumed that the data follow a continuous distribution, since dollar losses are measured on a ratio scale.
2. There is a small number of cases ($N < 25$).
3. The population standard deviation will be estimated using the pooled sample standard deviation.
4. The hypothesis being tested consists of comparing two means.

Hypothesis: The safety manager wishes to determine if the obtained plant average is significantly different from the company average. The null and alternative hypotheses are as follows:

Null Hypothesis: The sample mean is equal to the company average of $3,200.
Alternative Hypothesis: The sample mean is not equal to the company average of $3,200.

Decision Rule: The safety manager selected an α level of .05; therefore, since a two-tailed test is being conducted, she will reject the null hypothesis and accept the alternative if the obtained t is greater than ±2.02 (α = .05, df = 37). Since this is a two-tailed test, use the .025 column and because 37 does not appear in the degrees of freedom, the more conservative approach is to use the closest but higher number on the table. In this example, 40 degrees of freedom would be used.

Calculate t

The accident losses the safety manager obtained are as follows:

$2,500	$1,800	$2,700	$3,500	$900
$3,500	$2,200	$700	$5,600	$1,900
$5,200	$1,200	$3,700	$5,500	$1,800

To calculate *t*, the safety manager must determine the standard deviation and the average dollar loss per accident. Using the formulas provided in Chapter 4, the standard deviation was determined to be $1,614 and the mean $2,847. The variance was calculated to be $2,606,952.

The next step is to calculate the pooled standard deviation (S_p), *t*, and degrees of freedom. The results are as follows:

$$t = \frac{2,847 - 3,200}{1,605\sqrt{\frac{1}{15} + \frac{1}{24}}} = -.67$$

$$S_p = \sqrt{\frac{1,614^2(15-1) + 1,600^2(24-1)}{15 + 24 - 2}} = 1,605$$

$$df = 15 + 24 - 2 = 37$$

Conclusions: The obtained *t* score of –.67 is not greater than the critical score of 2.02, and therefore would not fall into the shaded area of the curve. The safety manager would accept the null hypothesis and conclude that the mean loss per vehicle accident for her plant is not significantly different from the company average.

Paired *t* Tests

The paired *t* test can be used to test hypotheses involving two means from paired observations. In this study, each subject is measured twice and the average differences between trial 1 and trial 2 are compared. These are also referred to as dependent observations. The hypotheses that can be tested include whether the differences between the two means are significantly greater, less than, or different from each other.

TEST ASSUMPTIONS

The assumptions that must be met to use the paired *t* test include the following (Witte and Witte 1997, 314–15):

1. There are two measures for each subject in the study.
2. The measures are continuous data.

HYPOTHESIS CONSTRUCTION

There are varieties of hypotheses that can be tested using the paired t test. Following is a summary of the hypotheses.

Null Hypothesis: The mean difference scores are equal to zero (no difference).
Alternative Hypothesis: The mean difference scores are not equal to zero (significantly different).

Null Hypothesis: The difference scores are greater than or equal to zero.
Alternative Hypothesis: The difference scores are less than zero.

Null Hypothesis: The difference scores are less than or equal to zero.
Alternative Hypothesis: The difference scores are greater than zero.

DETERMINE SIGNIFICANCE LEVELS

For each hypothesis tested, a critical score or cutoff region must be identified. This is done by using the hypothesis, the α level, and the degrees of freedom as was done in the previous t test. For a one-tailed test with an α level of .05, the critical region of the curve only appears at one end of the curve. For a two-tailed test, 2.5% lies at both ends of the curve and 95% in the middle. A t table is used to identify the critical score.

FORMULATE A DECISION RULE

The decision rule establishes the point at which the null hypothesis will be accepted or rejected. If the null hypothesis is rejected, then the alternative is accepted. For the one-tailed test, the decision rule would be to reject the null hypothesis and accept the alternative hypothesis if the obtained t score from the statistical test is greater than the critical score.

TEST FORMULA

The formula for calculating the paired t test is as follows (Witte and Witte 1997, 314–15):

$$t = \frac{\overline{D} - 0}{Sd / \sqrt{n}}$$

Where:

D Mean difference score
Sd Sample standard deviation score
n Number of paired observations
df n - 1

The sample standard deviation is calculated using the following formula:

$$Sd = \sqrt{\frac{n\Sigma D^2 - (\Sigma d)^2}{n(n-1)}}$$

CONCLUSIONS

The conclusions are reached by comparing the obtained t score to the cutoff score. If the obtained t score is greater than the cutoff score, then the null hypothesis is rejected and the alternative is accepted. The probability of incorrectly rejecting the null hypothesis (Type I Error) because of the results is equal to the α level.

EXAMPLE PAIRED t TEST PROBLEM

A training manager measured the test scores of 10 forklift drivers before and after a training program. He wanted to know if there were significant differences in the average before and after test scores for the subjects.

Assumptions: The data meet the assumptions for the paired t test because:

1. There are two measures for each subject in the study.
2. The measures are continuous data.
3. The hypothesis being tested consists of comparing two means.

Hypothesis: The training manager wishes to determine if there are significant differences in the average before and after test scores for the subjects. The null and alternative hypotheses are as follows:

Null Hypothesis: The average difference score is equal to 0.
Alternative Hypothesis: The average difference score is not equal to 0.

Decision Rule: The training manager selected an α level of .05, a two-tailed test is being conducted, and there are 9 degrees of freedom in this study ($n - 1$). The manager will reject the null hypothesis and accept the alternative if the obtained t is greater than ±2.262.

Calculate t

The data was collected and analyzed as follows:

Case	Test 1	Test 2	Score Difference	D2
1	78	83	5	25
2	76	91	15	225

(continued)

Case	Test 1	Test 2	Score Difference	D2
3	70	84	14	196
4	66	75	9	81
5	90	94	4	16
6	77	80	3	9
7	65	76	11	121
8	55	59	4	16
9	83	88	5	25
10	92	97	5	25
Total			75	739

The first step in the analysis is to calculate the standard deviation for the difference scores (S_d).

$$Sd = \sqrt{\frac{10(739) - (75)^2}{10(10-1)}} = 4.43$$

Next, t is calculated as

$$t = \frac{7.5 - 0}{4.43 / \sqrt{10}} = 5.36$$

Conclusions: The obtained t score of 5.36 is greater than the critical score of ±2.262 and would fall into the shaded area of the curve. Therefore, the training manager would reject the null hypothesis and conclude that the difference between the before and after scores for this sample is significantly greater than 0.

One-way Analysis of Variance

A one-way analysis of variance (ANOVA) procedure can be used to test hypotheses that compare more than two means. The ANOVA procedure uses an F ratio statistic to determine if there are significant differences between the means being tested. To determine where the significance lies between the means, follow-up or post hoc tests must be performed.

The ANOVA procedure makes comparisons about two different estimates of a population variance to test a hypothesis concerning the population mean: the within-group variance and the between-group variance. The within-group variance describes the variation of the data within each group of data, while the between-group variance describes the variation in the data from group to group. Together, these variances are used to derive the F ratio, which in turn is used to determine significance of the entire data set.

Table 6.1.   ANOVA Summary Table

Source of Variation	Sum of Squares	Df	Mean Squares	F Ratio
Between				
Within				
Total				

PROCEDURE ASSUMPTIONS

There are two major assumptions for an ANOVA procedure (Kirk 1982, 74–75). They are that:

1. The data within each group are continuous data and are normally distributed. This means that if a histogram of the data for each group were constructed, the histogram would form a bell-shaped curve.
2. The data are independent for each observation and for each group.

HYPOTHESIS CONSTRUCTION

In a one-way ANOVA, there are two variables for each observation. The first variable is the grouping variable. This variable is used to break the observations down into various groups, and then comparisons are made between them. The other variable is the continuous variable that is measured for each subject.

The null hypothesis for a one-way ANOVA is that there is no significant difference between means for the various groups of data. The alternative hypothesis is that there is a significant difference.

The ANOVA hypothesis for the three groups is as follows:

Null Hypothesis: The means for the three groups are equal.
Alternative Hypothesis: The means for the three groups are not equal.

PROCEDURE FORMULAS

The ANOVA procedure uses a standard format for presenting the results. A summary table is presented in Table 6.1.

As discussed previously, the comparisons between groups and within groups are used to form the F ratio. The sum of the between and within sum of squares yields the total sum of squares. Likewise, the between and within degrees of freedom yield the total degrees of freedom. The following steps are used to calculate a one-way ANOVA.

Step 1: Arrange the raw data table. The first step in calculating the ANOVA is to arrange the raw scores for each observation into a table.

Group 1	Group 2	Group 3
10	12	18
14	11	19
13	11	16
10	13	22
11	13	17

Step 2: Develop the null and alternative hypotheses.

Null Hypothesis: Mean of group 1 = Mean of group 2 = Mean of group 3 (All group means are equal).
Alternative Hypothesis: All group means are not equal.

Step 3: Calculate the group means and the grand mean. The averages for each group are calculated along with the overall grand mean for all observations.

	Group 1	Group 2	Group 3
	10	12	18
	14	11	19
	13	11	16
	10	13	22
	11	13	17
Group Total	58	60	92
Group Mean	11.6	12.0	18.4
Grand Mean	14.0		

Step 4: Calculate the between-group sum of squares. The between-group sum of squares is calculated by summing the squared deviations between each group. For each group, the number of cases in the group is multiplied by the squared difference between the group mean and the grand mean. The results for each group are summed to yield the between-group sum of squares.

The formula to calculate the between-group sum of squares is (Kuzma 1992, 147)

$$\text{SS between} = \Sigma \, n_i \, (X_i - \overline{X})^2$$

Using the data in the example, the following would be performed:

$$\text{SS}_{\text{between}} = 5(11.6 - 14)^2 + 5(12 - 14)^2 + 5(18.4 - 14)^2 = 145.6$$

Step 5: Calculate the total sum of squares. The total sum of squares is calculated by determining the sum of the squared deviation scores for each raw score from the grand mean using the following formula (Kuzma 1992, 147):

$$\text{SS total} = \Sigma \, \Sigma [(X_{ij} - \overline{X})^2]$$

Using the data in the example, the following would be performed:

$$SS_{total} = (10 - 14)^2 + (14 - 14)^2 + (13 - 14)^2 + (10 - 14)^2 + (11 - 14)^2$$
$$+ (12 - 14)^2 + (11 - 14)^2 + (11 - 14)^2 + (13 - 14)^2 + (13 - 14)^2 + (18$$
$$- 14)^2 + (19 - 14)^2 + (16 - 14)^2 + (22 - 14)^2 + (17 - 14)^2 = 184$$

Step 6: Calculate the sum of squares within. Because the sum of squares total is the sum of the sum of squares between plus within, one can derive the sum of squares within by subtracting the sum of squares between from the total sum of squares.

$$SS_{within} = SS_{total} - SS_{between}$$

Using the data in the example, the following would be performed:

$$SS_{within} = 184.0 - 145.6 = 38.4$$

Step 7: Calculate degrees of freedom. The degrees of freedom are calculated for the between sum of squares and the within sum of squares. Like the sum of squares, the sum of the between and within sum of squares yield the total sum of squares. The between degrees of freedom is the number of groups minus one, while the within degrees of freedom is the number of subjects minus the number of groups.

Within degrees of freedom = (number of subjects − number of groups)

Between degrees of freedom = (number of groups − 1)

Total degrees of freedom = (number of subjects − 1)

Using the data in the example, the following would be performed:

$$df_{between} = 3 - 1 = 2$$
$$df_{within} = 15 - 3 = 12$$
$$df_{total} = 15 - 1 = 14$$

Step 8: Calculate the mean squares. The mean squares (MS) are calculated by dividing the sum of squares by their respective degrees of freedom.

$$MS_{within} = SS_{within}/df_{within}$$
$$MS_{between} = SS_{between}/df_{between}$$

Using the data in the example, the following would be performed:

Table 6.2.   ANOVA Summary Table

Source of Variation	Sum of Squares	df	Mean Squares	F Ratio
Between	145.6	2	72.8	22.750
Within	38.4	12	3.2	
Total	184.0	14		

$$MS_{within} = 38.4/12 = 3.2$$

$$MS_{between} = 145.6/2 = 72.8$$

Step 9: Calculate the *F* ratio. The *F* ratio is calculated by dividing the mean squares between by mean squares within.

$$F \text{ ratio} = MS_{between}/MS_{within}$$

Using the data in the example, the following would be performed:

$$F \text{ ratio} = 72.8/3.2 = 22.75$$

Using all of the results computed in the previous steps, the completed one-way ANOVA table would appear as depicted in Table 6.2.

With the table completed, the statistical hypothesis testing and conclusions can now be reached.

HYPOTHESIS CONSTRUCTION

The researcher wishes to determine if there is a significant difference between the means for three groups. The null and alternative hypotheses are as follows:

Null Hypothesis: The means for the three groups are equal.
Alternative Hypothesis: The means for the three groups are not equal.

FORMULATE A DECISION RULE

The decision rule for ANOVA is based on the α level selected by the researcher and the degrees of freedom between and degrees of freedom within. With an α level of .05 and degrees of freedom of 2 and 12, the cutoff score is obtained from the *F* distribution table located in Appendix C. The table values are for an α level of .05. If the researcher wishes to select an α level of .01, he must use the *F* distribution table for the .01 level. The first column of the table is the within degrees of freedom, and the first row is the between degrees of freedom. For this example, the researcher would go down the first row to 12 and across the first column to 2. The number in the table at the intersection of these two points is the critical value, 3.89 on the 5% Critical Value F Table. If the obtained F ratio from the statistical procedure is greater than the table value, then the null hypothesis is rejected and the alternative is accepted.

CALCULATE F RATIO

The previous section covered in detail the procedure necessary to calculate the F ratio. The obtained F ratio for this example was 22.75.

CONCLUSIONS

The obtained F ratio of 22.75 is greater than the critical score of 3.89 and would fall into the shaded area of the curve. The researcher would reject the null hypothesis and conclude that the means for the three groups are significantly different from one another.

Post Hoc Procedures

The ANOVA procedure is used to determine whether means are significantly different from one another. It does not tell the researcher where the significance lies in regard to the specific means. For example, in the problem where three means were compared, the researcher cannot determine from the ANOVA if Group 1 is significantly different from Group 2 or if Group 2 is significantly different from Group 3 and so on. To make these determinations, a secondary test must be performed called a post hoc test. Post hoc tests are pairwise comparisons of means. To perform a post hoc test, a significant ANOVA must be obtained first.

Scheffe's Test

While the ANOVA procedure indicates a significant difference between group means, it does not indicate between which groups the significance lies. Post hoc tests compare the pairs of group means to answer this question. You must first obtain a significant ANOVA result before the post hoc tests can be used. There are many types of post hoc tests that can be performed. The major difference among the tests is the degree of difference in the pairs of means that must be found in order for the difference to be considered significant. One of the more conservative post hoc tests to run on the means is Scheffe's test, which tests not only pairwise comparisons but also all the a posteriori contrasts among means. To determine if a pair of means has significant differences, the absolute difference between the pair of means is compared to a critical value, Scheffe's test. The formula for calculating Scheffe's critical distance (CD) is as follows (Horvath 1974, 226–28):

$$CD = [q_{.05}(k, df MS_{error})] \sqrt{[n MS_{error}]}$$

CALCULATE SCHEFFE'S CD

The q term in the Scheffe's CD formula is obtained from the F distribution table using the number of groups and the degrees of freedom from the MS_{error} (within groups) terms. In this example, the critical F value at 3 and 12 degrees of freedom is 4.47 using the upper 2.5% F distribution table. Using the formula presented, Scheffe's S test was calculated as follows:

$$CD = [4.47]\sqrt{[(5)(3.2)]} = 17.88$$

FORMULATE A DECISION RULE

These absolute differences between the group totals are compared to Scheffe's CD to determine significance. If the absolute differences between the totals are greater than the CD value, then the two means are considered significantly different from one another. These significantly different means are noted in Table 6.3 with an asterisk.

EXAMPLE ANOVA PROBLEM

A safety manager wants to determine if there is a significant difference over a seven-month period in the mean number of accidents each month for three plants he manages.

Table 6.3. Significantly Different Means

	Group 1 58	Group 2 60	Group 3 92
Group 1 58	—	2	34*
Group 2 60		—	32*
Group 3 92			—

Step 1: Arrange the raw data table.

Plant A	Plant B	Plant C
3	4	7
2	7	9
3	9	8
4	5	6
6	8	4
5	5	7
3	8	3

Step 2: Develop the null and alternative hypotheses.

Null Hypothesis: All group means are equal.
Alternative Hypothesis: All group means are not equal.

Step 3: Calculate the group means and the grand mean. The averages for each group are calculated, along with the overall grand mean for all observations.

	Plant A	Plant B	Plant C
	3	4	7
	2	7	9
	3	9	8
	4	5	6
	6	8	4
	5	5	7
	3	8	3
Group Mean	3.71	6.57	6.29
Grand Mean	5.52		

Step 4: Calculate the between-group sum of squares.

$SS_{between} = 7(3.71 - 5.52)^2 + 7(6.57 - 5.52)^2 + 7(6.29 - 5.52)^2 = 34.67$

Step 5: Calculate the total sum of squares.

$SS_{total} = (3 - 5.52)^2 + (2 - 5.52)^2 + (3 - 5.52)^2 + (4 - 5.52)^2 + (6 - 5.52)^2 + (5 - 5.52)^2 + (3 - 5.52)^2 + (4 - 5.52)^2 + (7 - 5.52)^2 + (9 - 5.52)^2 + (5 - 5.52)^2 + (8 - 5.52)^2 + (5 - 5.52)^2 + (8 - 5.52)^2 + (7 - 5.52)^2 + (9 - 5.52)^2 + (8 - 5.52)^2 + (6 - 5.52)^2 + (4 - 5.52)^2 + (7 - 5.52)^2 + (3 - 5.52)^2 = 95.24$

Step 6: Calculate the sum of squares within.

$$SS_{within} = 95.24 - 34.67 = 60.57$$

Step 7: Calculate degrees of freedom.

$$df_{within} = 21 - 3 = 18$$

$$df_{between} = 3 - 1 = 2$$

$$df_{total} = 21 - 1 = 20$$

Step 8: Calculate the mean squares. The mean squares are calculated by dividing the sum of squares by their respective degrees of freedom.

$$MS_{within} = SS_{within}/df_{within}$$

$$MS_{between} = SS_{between}/df_{between}$$

Using the data in the example, the following would be performed:

$$MS_{within} = 60.57/18 = 3.37$$

$$MS_{between} = 34.67/2 = 17.33$$

Step 9: Calculate the *F* Ratio. The *F* ratio is calculated by dividing the mean squares between by mean squares within.

$$F \text{ ratio} = MS_{between}/MS_{within}$$

Using the data in the example, the following would be performed:

$$F \text{ ratio} = 17.33/3.37 = 5.10$$

Using all of the results completed in the previous steps, the completed one-way ANOVA table would appear as depicted in Table 6.4.

With the completed table, the statistical hypothesis testing and conclusions can now be reached.

Hypothesis: The researcher wishes to determine if there is a significant difference between the means for the three groups. The null and alternative hypotheses are as follows:

Null Hypothesis: The means for the three groups are equal.
Alternative Hypothesis: The means for the three groups are not equal.

Table 6.4. ANOVA Summary Table

Source of Variation	Sum of Squares	df	Mean Squares	F Ratio
Between	34.67	2	17.33	5.14
Within	60.57	18	3.37	
Total	95.24	20		

FORMULATE A DECISION RULE

The decision rule for ANOVA is based on the α level selected by the researcher and the degrees of freedom between and the degrees of freedom within. With an α level of .05 and degrees of freedom of 2 and 18, the cutoff score obtained from the F distribution table is 3.55.

CALCULATE F RATIO

The obtained F ratio for this example was 5.14.

CONCLUSIONS

The obtained F ratio of 5.10 is greater than the critical score of 3.55 and would fall into the shaded area of the curve. The researcher would reject the null hypothesis and conclude that the means for the three groups are significantly different from one another.

Chapter Summary

There are many statistical tests available to researchers for the purpose of testing hypotheses that compare means. The basic comparisons are those that compare two means. An assumption of normality must be met to use the z test. If this assumption cannot be met, then the t test is an alternative. More complex hypotheses concerning means include t tests for paired comparisons and the ANOVA procedure.

The one-way ANOVA procedure can be used to determine if there are significant differences in mean values across groups in a sample. Using the F ratio and F distribution to determine significance, post hoc procedures must be used to determine exactly where the significant difference lies between pairs of means.

Chapter Review Exercises

1. Describe the situations in which a researcher would choose the z test over a t test.
2. Provide an example of a null and alternative hypothesis for each of the following procedures.

    z test ($N > 25$); t test ($N < 25$); one-way ANOVA

3. What critical score should a researcher use if he is running a z test for the following null and alternative hypotheses (assuming α level = .05)?

    Null Hypothesis: The mean difference scores are equal to zero (no difference).
    Alternative Hypothesis: The mean difference scores are not equal to zero (significantly different).

4. What critical score should a researcher use if he is running a t test for the following null and alternative hypotheses (assuming α level = .05 and df = 30)?

Null Hypothesis: The difference scores are greater than or equal to zero.
Alternative Hypothesis: The difference scores are less than zero.

5. What information is used to determine the critical score for a one-way ANOVA?

6. A trainer wishes to compare the average test score for his class to the national averages. The trainer believes his class scored significantly higher than the average. The national average is 86% (SD = 10, N = 100), and his class scored 94%, with a standard deviation of 3.0. Assume an α level of .05 and a sample size of 50. Provide the hypothesis being tested, the rejection rule, the results, and the decision that one should make on the basis of the results.

7. A training manager collected data from a group of 10 subjects. Each subject was observed and the number of unsafe acts was recorded. The subjects then participated in a safety awareness training program. They were again observed, and the unsafe acts recorded. How would the manager set up a statistical test to determine if there were any changes in the unsafe acts observed?

8. A safety manager wanted to determine if there was a significant difference in the average number of accidents before lunch than after. He compared the average number of accidents of two groups of employees. The manager recorded the number of accidents for 20 employees before lunch and 20 different employees after lunch. Each month, one group averaged 2 accidents, with a standard deviation of 0.03 before lunch, while the other group averaged 3 accidents, with a standard deviation of 0.15 after lunch. Are there significantly more accidents for the after-lunch group? Provide the hypothesis being tested, the rejection rule, the results, and the decision that one should make on the basis of the results. Use an α level of .05.

9. An environmental researcher believed that there were significantly different blood lead levels for children living in three different buildings in a housing complex. The researcher ran an ANOVA procedure and obtained the following results:

Source of Variation	df	Sum of Squares	Mean Squares	F
Between	2	14,230	7,115	1.74
Within	9	36,720	4,080	
Total	11	50,950		

Provide the seven steps for the analysis. What conclusions should be drawn from this study?

10. What t score would give a researcher 10% of the population at each end of the curve and 80% of the cases in the middle section (assume df = 24)?

11. A researcher was performing a one-way ANOVA. He identified the df_{within} to be 15 and the $df_{between}$ to be 4. What is the critical score, assuming the α level = .05?

CHAPTER 7

Correlation and Regression

Correlation

Correlation procedures are used to indicate a measure of association (i.e., some relation) between two or more variables (Horvath 1974, 252). Although a correlation does not necessarily imply cause and effect, it is often incorrectly interpreted as implying a cause-and-effect relation. An experiment is needed to show a cause-and-effect relation.

There are various correlation procedures available. The procedure used depends on the format of the data. When two variables are being correlated, it is referred to as bivariate correlation. When more than two variables are used, it is referred to as multiple correlation.

The two variables of bivariate correlation are the dependent variable and the independent variable. The independent variable influences the dependent variable, and the correlation coefficient is a measure of this association. Each subject or case in a correlation procedure is measured by the two variables. One can graph the cases in what is called a scatterplot to depict the relation. A scatterplot is set up with the independent variable along the horizontal x-axis and the dependent variable along the vertical y-axis. Each point on the scatterplot represents one case.

The result of a correlation procedure is the correlation coefficient, which can be represented by r. The correlation coefficient indicates the strength of the association between the variables and the type of association present. Correlation coefficients run along a continuum from -1.00 to $+1.00$, with 0 as the midpoint. A correlation coefficient of -1.00 is referred to as a perfect inverse correlation, while a correlation coefficient of $+1.00$ is referred to as a perfect positive correlation. With a negative or inverse correlation, the y variable decreases as the x variable increases. With a positive correlation the y variable increases as the x variable increases. Figure 7.1 depicts the positive and negative correlation coefficients.

Scatterplot A represents a positive correlation. As the values along the horizontal axis increase, the corresponding values on the vertical axis also increase. Scatterplot B, on the other hand, represents a negative or inverse relation. As the values on the horizontal axis increase, the corresponding values on the vertical axis decrease.

81

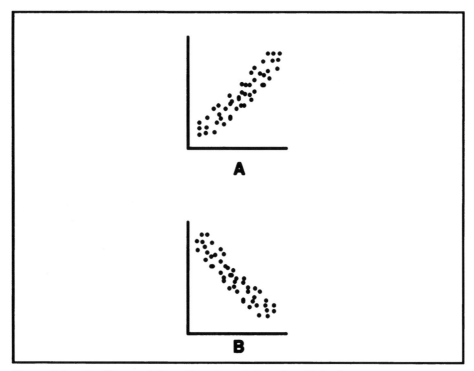

Figure 7.1.   Positive and Negative Correlation Coefficients

Scatterplots can also be used to depict the strength of the correlation or relation between two variables. As the correlation coefficient nears 0, this is referred to as having no correlation or relation. The points on a scatterplot in this case tend to appear as a cloud with no real pattern toward either a positive or a negative correlation. In Figure 7.2, scatterplot A represents a weak correlation.

Moving away from the 0 in either direction, the strength of the association increases. As the points on a scatterplot approach a straight line, the correlation coefficient approaches 1.00. Scatterplot B represents a strong negative correlation. Scatterplots that range between a perfectly straight line and a circular cloud can then represent correlations between 0 and 1.00. Scatterplot C depicts a moderate positive correlation.

Another measure for the correlation coefficient is r^2. Squaring the correlation coefficient gives the researcher an indication of the amount of variability in the dependent variable that can be directly attributed to the independent variable. This is referred to as the coefficient of determination. For example, if a correlation coefficient of .75 was obtained from a correlation procedure, then $.75^2$ or 56% of the variability in the dependent variable can be attributed to the independent variable.

PEARSON CORRELATION COEFFICIENT

There are a number of bivariate correlation procedures. The differences in the procedures are due to differences in the format of the data being used. For example, if one

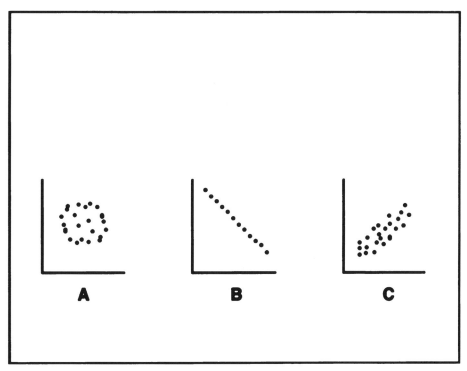

Figure 7.2.   Strengths of the correlation coefficients

wishes to correlate two variables where both are continuous in nature, then the Pearson correlation coefficient can be used. Table 7.1 shows data formats with the type of correlation coefficient that should be used with each.

As stated above, the Pearson correlation procedure is used when both variables are continuous in nature. In addition to this requirement, the following assumptions must be met in order to use the Pearson correlation coefficient (Horvath 1974, 255–56):

Assumptions

1. Each case is independent of the other.
2. Each variable assumes a normal distribution.
3. Each variable is measured on either an interval scale or a ratio scale.

Table 7.1.   Data Formats and Correlation Procedures

Dependent Variable	Independent Variable	Procedure
Interval/ratio	Interval/ratio	Pearson correlation coefficient
Ordinal	Ordinal	Spearman rank–order correlation coefficient
Dichotomous	Dichotomous	Phi coefficient
Interval	Categorical	Eta coefficient
Interval	Dichotomous	Point biserial correlation

Formula

The following formula is used to calculate the Pearson correlation coefficient (Kuzma 1992, 200):

$$r = \frac{\Sigma xy - \frac{(\Sigma x)(\Sigma y)}{n}}{\sqrt{\left[\Sigma x^2 - \frac{(\Sigma x)^2}{n}\right]\left[\Sigma y^2 - \frac{(\Sigma y)^2}{n}\right]}}$$

Sample Problem

Data was obtained from six subjects who experienced serious back injuries while on the job. The safety director wanted to determine if there was a relation between the total costs for the injuries and the number of years employed in a manual material handling job. The data obtained was as follows:

Case	Injury Experience ($1,000) (y)	y^2	Years on the Job (x)	x^2	xy
1	23	529	12	144	276
2	34	1,156	16	256	544
3	65	4,225	14	196	910
4	76	5,776	12	144	912
5	54	2,916	20	400	1,080
6	56	3,136	15	225	840
Sum	308	17,738	89	1,365	4,562

Putting the above numbers into the formula, we get

$$r = \frac{4,562 - \frac{(89)(308)}{6}}{\sqrt{\left[1,365 - \frac{(89)^2}{6}\right]\left[17,738 - \frac{(308)^2}{6}\right]}} = -.023$$

The results indicate that there is a weak inverse relation between the number of years on the job and the severity as measured in dollars for back injuries.

SPEARMAN RANK–ORDER CORRELATION COEFFICIENT

The Spearman rank–order correlation coefficient is used to determine correlations between ranked or ordinal data (Kuzma 1992, 225–26).

Assumptions

The procedure requires that the same items be ranked by two different judges. It then determines the degree of association between the two sets of rankings. A significant positive correlation signifies that both judges were in agreement with the rankings, while a significant negative correlation signifies that one judge ranked the items lowest to highest while the other ranked them highest to lowest.

Formula

The following formula is used to calculate the Spearman rank–order correlation coefficient (Kuzma 1992, 225):

$$r_s = 1 - \frac{6 \, \Sigma d^2}{n \, (n^2 - 1)}$$

Sample Problem

Two judges were asked to rank five teams from best to worst, with 1 being best and 5 being worst. A researcher wanted to determine the correlation between the two judges' rankings. The following table was constructed in order to analyze the data. Difference scores were calculated by subtracting Judge 2's rankings from Judge 1's rankings. The differences were then squared.

Football Team	Poll 1 Rankings	Poll 2 Rankings	Difference	Difference Squared
Ohio	1	2	−1	1
Nebraska	2	1	1	1
Florida	3	3	0	0
Pennsylvania	4	5	−1	1
Michigan	5	4	1	1
Sum				4

The data from the table were entered into the formula, yielding the following results:

$$r_s = 1 - \frac{6 \, (4)}{5 \, (5^2 - 1)} = .80$$

The results can be interpreted as a strong relation between the judges' rankings for the items in this study.

PHI COEFFICIENT

The Phi coefficient (ϕ) is used to rank two dichotomous variables. A dichotomous variable is one that has only two possible outcomes, such as yes/no, male/female, etc. (Cohen and Cohen 1983, 39).

Assumptions

The procedure requires that both variables have only two possible outcomes.

Formula

The frequency of cases is displayed in a two-by-two table, with the cells in the table being represented by the following letters:

	Males	Females	Total
Yes	A	B	A + B
No	C	D	C + D
Total	A + C	B + D	A + B + C + D

The following formula is used to calculate the phi coefficient (Cohen and Cohen 1983, 39).

$$r_\phi = \frac{BC - AD}{\sqrt{(A+B)(C+D)(A+C)(B+D)}}$$

Sample Problem

Using the frequencies from the cells in the table, it is just a matter of calculating the correlation coefficient.

	Males	Females	Total
Yes	10	6	16
No	8	15	23
Total	18	21	39

$$r_\phi = \frac{(6)(8) - (15)(10)}{\sqrt{(10+6)(8+15)(10+8)(6+15)}} = -.27$$

η COEFFICIENT

The η coefficient provides an estimate of the degree of association between a nominal variable grouped by an interval variable. The η correlation coefficient can be calculated using the sum of squares between groups and the total sum of squares from the ANOVA procedure (Kirk 1982, 162).

Formula

The η coefficient is calculated as follows (Kirk 1982, 162):

$$\text{Eta}^2 = \frac{\text{SS Between} - (p-1)\text{MS Within}}{\text{SS Total} + \text{MS Within}}$$

Where
p = Number of groups.

The result from the η procedure is interpreted in the same manner as the squared correlation coefficient.

Sample Problem

In Chapter 6 we used an example where a safety manager wanted to determine if there was a significant difference for three plants over a seven-month period in the mean number of accidents each month. An ANOVA procedure was performed to answer this question, yielding the following results table:

Source of Variation	Sum of Squares	df	Mean Squares	F Ratio
Between	34.67	2	17.33	5.15
Within	60.57	18	3.4	
Total	95.24	20		

The η coefficient can be calculated using the information from the ANOVA as follows:

$$\text{Eta}^2 = \frac{34.67 - (2)(3.4)}{95.24 + 3.4} = .28$$

The result from the η procedure is interpreted in the same manner as the squared correlation coefficient. The result of .28 indicates that 28% of the variability in the dependent variable can be attributed to the independent variable.

POINT BISERIAL CORRELATION

The point biserial correlation coefficient provides an estimate of the degree of association between an interval grouped by a dichotomous variable.

Assumptions

The assumption is that each subject is measured by a dichotomous variable that represents the independent variable and one interval variable that represents the dependent variable.

Formula

The formula for calculating the point biserial correlation coefficient is (Cohen and Cohen 1983, 27–39)

$$r_{pb} = \frac{(\overline{Y}_1 - \overline{Y}_2)\sqrt{pq}}{sd_y}$$

Where:
$\overline{Y}_1$ Average Y for subjects categorized in group 1
$\overline{Y}_2$ Average Y for subjects categorized in group 0
p   Proportion of subjects in group 0
q   Proportion of subjects in group 1
sdy   Population standard deviation

Sample Problem

An investigator collected data from a group of subjects that consisted of 10 males and 10 females. The data were ergonomic analysis surveys and each subject received an overall job satisfaction score. The investigator wanted to determine if there was a relation between the scores and the gender of the respondent.

To answer this question, the investigator chose the Point Biserial Correlation Coefficient. The data were as follows:

Case	Male	Female
1	54	87
2	55	76
3	56	56
4	58	77
5	67	98
6	78	65
7	76	64
8	67	58
9	89	87
10	92	88
Average	69.2	75.6

The standard deviation for the entire data set was calculated to be 14.2 using the formulas presented previously in Chapter 4. The proportion of males in this study was 50%, as was the proportion for females.

$$r_{pb} = \frac{(69.2 - 75.6)\sqrt{(.50)(.50)}}{14.2} = -.23$$

The result from the point biserial correlation procedure is interpreted in the same manner as a correlation coefficient, with –.23 representing a weak negative correlation.

SIGNIFICANCE TESTING FOR CORRELATION COEFFICIENTS

Thus far, we have only shown how to determine the correlation coefficients for two variables and how, using the coefficient, an understanding of the strength of the correlation between the variables, whether positive or negative, can be gained. The next step is to determine if the relation between the variables is significant.

Test Hypotheses

The significance test for correlation coefficients uses the t test. It tests the hypothesis that the correlation coefficient is significantly different from 0, meaning that there is no relation present. The same process used with other t tests is followed.

Null Hypothesis: The correlation coefficient equals 0.
Alternative Hypothesis: The correlation coefficient is not equal to 0.

It is important to keep in mind that although a correlation may be significant, the researcher must also use some judgment as to the importance by examining the coefficient of determination as well. For example, a correlation coefficient of .04 could very well be found to be significant; however, the researcher can only account for less than .2% ($.04^2$) of the variability in the dependent variable using that particular independent variable.

Test Formula

The formula for testing the significance of a correlation coefficient is derived using the following (Cohen and Cohen 1983, 52–53):

$$t = \frac{r}{(1-r^2)/(n-2)}$$

$$df = n-2$$

Sample Problem

In the example used in this chapter in the section on Pearson correlation coefficient, a correlation coefficient of $-.23$ was obtained for 6 cases when examining the relation between years on the job and severity of back injuries as measured by loss. To determine if the correlation is significant, the following hypothesis was tested:

Null Hypothesis: The correlation coefficient is equal to 0.
Alternative Hypothesis: The correlation coefficient is not equal to 0.

The t test that tests this hypothesis is as follows:

$$t = \frac{-.23}{(1 - -.23^2)/(6-2)} = -.47$$

df = 6 - 2 = 4

Using the t table, a critical value of 2.77 was obtained for a two-tailed test and an α level of .05. The obtained t is less than the critical score; therefore, the researcher must accept the null hypothesis and conclude that the correlation coefficient is not significant.

Regression

Regression procedures allow a person to develop prediction equations that can be used to predict dependent variables from independent variables. With regression, a correlation coefficient is first derived. Then an equation for the line that best fits the data points is calculated. The formula for the line that describes the regression is given by

$$y = bx + a$$

Where b represents the slope of the line and a represents the y intercept for the line. Similar to that in correlations, x represents the independent variable and y represents the dependent variable. The slope of the line is the rise of the line over the run. Figure 7.3 depicts the equation of a line.

To predict a new y variable from an x, plug the x into the equation to yield the expected y. In a given example, a prediction equation of $y = .32x + 10$ was obtained. The expected y from an x of 20 would be 16.4 [$y = .32(20) + 10$].

ASSUMPTIONS

The assumptions for the regression are the same as for the Pearson correlation coefficient.

1. Each case is independent of the other.
2. Each variable assumes a normal distribution.
3. Each variable is measured on at least the interval scale or ratio scale.

FORMULAS

The first step is to calculate the equation of a line, $y = bx + a$ (Cohen and Cohen 1983, 41–43). The slope of the line, b, is calculated using the following formula:

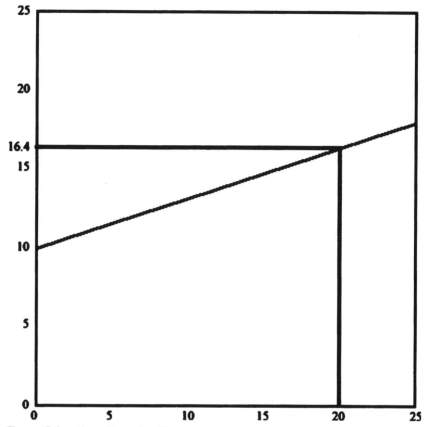

Figure 7.3.   Equation of a Line

$$b = r\frac{Sdy}{Sdx}$$

Where:
r = Pearson correlation coefficient
SD_x = Standard deviation of x
SD_y = Standard deviation of y

The y intercept, a, is calculated using the means of both variables with the following formula:

$$a = \overline{Y} - b\overline{X}$$

SAMPLE PROBLEM

A safety manager wanted to determine if there was a significant relation between the number of hours of training an employee completed and the severity of injury the employee received while on the job. Because both variables are continuous, the Pearson correlation coefficient would be appropriate. The data, collected over a one-month period, are arranged in the following table.

Case	Losses ($) (y)	y^2	Hours of Training (x)	x^2	xy
1	$10	$100	15	225	$150
2	$9	$81	26	676	$234
3	$1	$1	54	2916	$54
4	$2	$4	40	1600	$80
5	$13	$169	18	324	$234
Sum	$35	$355	153	5741	$752
SD	$05.24		16.27		
Average	$7		30.6		

Step 1: Calculate the Pearson correlation coefficient.

$$r = \frac{752 - \frac{(153)(35)}{5}}{\sqrt{\left[355 - \frac{(35)^2}{5}\right]\left[5.741 - \frac{(153)^2}{5}\right]}} = -.93$$

A correlation coefficient of −.93 was obtained, indicating that there is a strong inverse relation between the number of hours of training and the severity of the injury. As the hours of training increase, the severity of injury decreases.

The next step is to determine if the correlation coefficient is significant. To do this, a *t* test is performed on the correlation coefficient. The null hypothesis tested is that the correlation coefficient is equal to 0. If the *t* test is significant, the null hypothesis is rejected and the alternative, *r* is not equal to 0, is accepted.

Step 2: Determine the significance of r.

$$t = \frac{-.93}{(1 - -.93^2)/(5-2)} = -4.38$$

$$df = 5 - 2 = 3$$

Using the *t* table, the critical score for *t* with 3 degrees of freedom is ±3.18. The obtained *t* is −4.38; therefore the *t* score falls in the shaded area of the curve. The null hypothesis is rejected and the alternative is accepted. The researcher would conclude that there is a significant correlation between the number of hours of training and the average first-aid claim.

Step 3: With a significant r, *calculate the equation of the line.*

The next step is to calculate the regression equation for this data. The following formulas are used to calculate the equation of a line, $y = bx + a$.

$$b = \frac{(-.93)(5.24)}{16.27} = -.30$$

$$a = 7 - (-.30)(30.6) = 16.18$$

$$Y = -.30X + 16.18$$

Step 4: Use the equation of the line to predict dependent variables from independent variables.

The researcher can then use the equation to predict the dependent variable from independent variables. For example, if the researcher wanted to determine the predicted dollar loss for someone with 35 hours of training, he would insert 35 in the equation and solve for *y*.

$$y = -.30(35) + 16.18$$
$$y = 5.68$$

The equation yields 5.68, meaning that based on the prior data, if a person received 35 hours of training, he or she would be expected to incur $5.68 in first-aid losses.

Chapter Summary

Correlation procedures are widely used in research studies; however, they can be easily misinterpreted. Correlations indicate the strength and type of relation that exists between variables. Correlations do not indicate cause and effect, but are many times misinterpreted as doing so.

When using correlation procedures, one must select the procedure based upon the type of data used in the study. Also, a strong correlation coefficient does not necessarily mean a significant relation. Consequently, a significant correlation coefficient does not necessarily mean the correlation is important. This is the case when there is a significant but extremely weak correlation coefficient.

The regression procedure can be used to predict a dependent variable from a known independent variable. The prediction equation is formulated using the results of previously obtained data. Using a regression equation, the researcher can obtain expected values for a dependent variable. Although one may be able to generate a regression equation from a set of data, the strength of the correlation coefficient plays an important role in determining the accuracy of the regression equation and its usefulness in predicting.

Chapter Review Exercises

1. What are the data requirements for using the Pearson correlation procedure?
2. What are the data requirements for using the point biserial correlation procedure?

3. Define dependent variable and independent variable. Why is knowing this important?
4. What is regression used for?
5. How would one interpret a correlation coefficient of .80 compared to −.80?
6. An investigator obtained a correlation coefficient of .60. What must be done to determine if this is significant?
7. Describe the relation between correlation coefficients, significance tests, and the coefficient of determination and why all three are important when making decisions concerning correlation coefficients.
8. Subjects were asked to complete a Cumulative Trauma Disorder (CTD) scale (high score represents many CTD symptoms, low score represents few CTD symptoms) and to disclose how many times they missed work each month. The following descriptive statistics were obtained:

Variance of x = 155
Variance of y = .40
Mean of x = 65
Mean of y = 2.7
r = .62

If there were 200 subjects in this study, would the correlation coefficient be significant?
9. A regression equation was calculated on safety training scores and the number of safety infractions in one year. The equation derived was as follows:

$$y = .09x + 1.02$$

What is the expected number of safety infractions of someone with a safety training score of 27?
10. A safety manager wished to determine if there was a relation between the department employees belonged to and their subjective rating for wrist pain using a ten-point scale (1, little or no pain, to 10, severe pain). The following data were collected:

Case	Department A	Department B
1	2	7
2	4	6
3	5	8
4	3	9
5	2	10
6	5	7
7	4	5
8	6	6
9	3	6
10	2	4
11	4	7

Case	Department A	Department B
12	1	4
13	3	3
14	5	7
15	3	8

Is there a relation between department membership and subjective pain levels?

CHAPTER 8

Nonparametric Statistics

Underlying Assumptions Concerning Nonparametric Statistics

Nonparametric statistics are used when the data cannot be assumed to follow a particular distribution. These tests are also referred to as distribution-free tests (Hays 1988, 814–15). Nonparametric statistics are typically used with ordinal and categorical data.

Chi-square Test for Goodness of Fit

Chi-square (χ^2) tests are used with categorical data and assume a χ^2 distribution. χ^2 tests for goodness of fit determine if obtained proportions in a sample are significantly different from what would be expected owing to chance (Hays 1988, 768–71). The frequencies of cases are obtained for a series of possible outcomes. The obtained frequencies are then compared to the expected frequencies for significant differences. If there are significant differences between the obtained frequencies and the expected frequencies, then the test results would be considered significant.

DEGREES OF FREEDOM

Used on categorical data, a χ^2 distribution takes into account the changes in probabilities due to changes in sample size. This is done through what are called degrees of freedom, which can be thought of as a sample's freedom to vary in obtained scores (Hays 1988, 294). Given a known variance for the population, all scores can vary except one. So in a population of 10 subjects, when summing all deviations, the sum must be zero. With this known, nine scores can be anything, but the last must be of a value that causes the deviation to equal zero. With tests such as the χ^2, sample size affects the expected test value. As the degrees of freedom change, so does the shape of the χ^2 distribution and the critical values.

TEST ASSUMPTIONS

Data are categorical in nature and the frequency of cases or subjects are identified for each category.

HYPOTHESIS CONSTRUCTION

Null Hypothesis: Observed frequency of cases in the cells equals expected frequency of cases in the cells.

Alternative Hypothesis: Observed frequency of cases in the cells does not equal expected frequency of cases in the cells.

TEST FORMULA

The test formula for the χ^2 goodness of fit test is as follows (Hays 1988, 771):

$$X^2 = \Sigma \left[\frac{(\text{observed - expected})^2}{\text{expected}} \right]$$

The degrees of freedom for this test are calculated using the relation (Number of Groups – 1).

DETERMINE CRITICAL VALUE

The critical value is determined by using the χ^2 distribution table for the appropriate α level and the degrees of freedom. The χ^2 table is located in the Appendix of this book. In this table, the degrees of freedom are located in the first column and the α levels are located in the first row. To find the critical value, the point at which these two meet has to be noted.

SAMPLE PROBLEM

A die was rolled 120 times and the number of times each side came up was recorded. From this information, the following table was developed:

Value	Observed
1	15
2	18
3	22
4	21
5	24
6	20
Total	120

Step 1: Hypothesis construction

Null Hypothesis: Observed frequency of cases in the cells equals expected frequency of cases in the cells.

Alternative Hypothesis: Observed frequency of cases in the cells does not equal expected frequency of cases in the cells.

Step 2: Statistical test

Because the data are categorical in nature and the cases are frequencies, the χ^2 test of goodness of fit is the appropriate statistical test.

Step 3: Determine the critical value

The table is a single array of numbers with six possible outcomes; therefore there are 5 (6 – 1) degrees of freedom. The researcher has selected an α level of .05; therefore, on using the χ^2 table for five degrees of freedom and an α level of .05, the critical value is 11.07. The decision rule would be to reject the null hypothesis and accept the alternative hypothesis if the obtained χ^2 is greater than the critical value of 11.07.

Step 4: Calculate the χ^2

To calculate the χ^2, the researcher must first determine the expected number of cases for each cell. In 120 rolls, one would expect that, in a totally random situation, each side of the die would come up 20 times. According to this assumption, the observed number of rolls for each side of the die is compared to what is expected. If there is a significant difference between the observed and expected number of rolls, the results would be considered significant. The following table of observed and expected outcomes for the rolls was developed:

Value	Observed	Expected
1	15	20
2	18	20
3	22	20
4	21	20
5	24	20
6	20	20
Total	120	120

This formula requires that for each possible outcome, the observed frequency of cases be compared to the expected.

$$\chi^2 = \frac{(15-20)^2}{20} + \frac{(18-20)^2}{20} + \frac{(22-20)^2}{20} + \frac{(21-20)^2}{20} +$$

$$\frac{(24-20)^2}{20} + \frac{(20-20)^2}{20} = 2.50$$

The degrees of freedom are equal to (Number of Groups – 1); therefore, there are 5 degrees of freedom for this test (6 – 1). Using the χ^2 table, the critical value for an α level of .05 and 5 degrees of freedom is 11.07.

Step 5: Decision rule

The obtained χ^2 value of 2.50 is not greater than 11.07; therefore the null hypothesis is not rejected. The researcher concludes that the observed frequency of cases is not significantly different from what was expected.

χ^2 Test of Association

The χ^2 test of association can be used with data in which each subject is measured by two categorical variables. The test assumes a χ^2 distribution. The statistical procedure follows the same type of process as does the χ^2 goodness of fit test, in which the observed frequency of cases in each cell is compared to an expected number. The observed frequencies in each cell are then compared to the frequencies that were expected for significance.

DEGREES OF FREEDOM

The degrees of freedom for the χ^2 test of association are determined by the following formula:

$$df = (\text{Number of Rows} - 1) \times (\text{Number of Columns} - 1)$$

EXPECTED NUMBER OF CASES

In the χ^2 goodness of fit test, the expected number for each cell was determined by dividing the total number of subjects by the total number of cells (Hays 1988, 777). This is done because there was an assumption that each person had an equally likely chance of falling into any one of the cells. In the χ^2 test of association, since we are dealing with tables with multiple cells, we cannot assume an equally likely chance of falling into each cell because the proportions of the population may not follow this assumption. Therefore, to calculate the expected number in a particular cell of the table, one would use the following formula:

$$\text{Expected Number of Cases} = \frac{\text{Row Total} \times \text{Column Total}}{\text{Grand Total}}$$

The row total in which that particular cell lies in the table and the column total where that particular cell lies would be used to calculate the expected number for that particular cell.

TEST ASSUMPTIONS

Data are categorical in nature and the frequency of cases or subjects is identified for each category.

HYPOTHESIS CONSTRUCTION

Null Hypothesis: Observed frequency of cases in the cells equals the expected frequency of cases in the cells.

Alternative Hypothesis: Observed frequency of cases in the cells does not equal the expected frequency of cases in the cells.

TEST FORMULA

The following formula is used to calculate the χ^2 of association (Hays 1988, 775–77):

$$\chi^2 = \Sigma \left[\frac{(\text{observed} - \text{expected})^2}{\text{expected}} \right]$$

df = (Number of Rows − 1)(Number of Columns − 1)

Sample Problem

A group of subjects was categorized by gender and voter registration. The following table was developed:

Registered	Male	Female
Yes	23	240
No	450	76

The researcher would like to know if there is a significant relationship between these variables.

Step 1: Hypothesis construction

Null Hypothesis: Observed frequency of cases in the cells equals the expected frequency of cases in the cells.

Alternative Hypothesis: Observed frequency of cases in the cells does not equal the expected frequency of cases in the cells.

Step 2: Statistical test

Because the data are categorical in nature and the cases are frequencies, the χ^2 test of association is the appropriate statistical test.

Step 3: Determine the critical value

The table is a 3-by-2 table; therefore there are $(3 - 1)(2 - 1) = 2$ degrees of freedom. The researcher has selected an α level of .05. Using the χ^2 table for 2 degrees of freedom and an α level of .05, the critical value is 5.99. The decision rule would be to reject the null hypothesis and accept the alternative hypothesis if the obtained χ^2 is greater than the critical value of 5.99.

Step 4: Calculate χ^2

To calculate the χ^2, the researcher must first determine the expected number of cases for each cell. In the cell for "Males" and "Yes," the expected number of cases would be equal to $(263 \times 473)/789$ or 158. This process is followed for all cells in the table.

Observed Cases

Registered	Male	Female	Total
Yes	23	240	263
No	450	76	526
Total	473	316	789

Expected Cases

Registered	Male	Female	Total
Yes	158	105	263
No	315	211	526
Total	473	316	789

The following formula was used to calculate the χ^2:

$$\chi^2 = \frac{(23 - 158)^2}{158} + \frac{(240 - 105)^2}{105} + \frac{(450 - 315)^2}{315} + \frac{(76 - 211)^2}{211}$$

$$\chi^2 = 433$$

Step 5: Decision rule

The obtained χ^2 value of 433 is greater than 5.99; therefore the null hypothesis is rejected and the alternative is accepted. The researcher concludes that the observed frequency of cases is significantly different from what was expected and there is a relationship between gender and voting.

Wilcoxon Rank-Sum Test

The Wilcoxon rank-sum test determines whether there are significant differences between sets of ranks (Horvath 1974, 337–38). The rankings are compared for two sets of independent populations. If there is a significant Wilcoxon rank-sum test result, one can conclude that there are significant differences in the sum of the ranks when comparing the two groups.

TEST ASSUMPTIONS

To calculate the Wilcoxon rank sum, the researcher must first rank all subjects from lowest to highest. For each group, the sum of the ranks is computed, then the average rank. To determine the critical value for the z test, the researcher uses the normal distribution table for the appropriate α level and a two-tailed test. If, for example, the α level was .05, the critical score would be ±1.96.

Next, the expected rank for the groups is calculated and compared with the observed sum of the ranks. A z test is performed to determine if the difference between the observed and expected results is significant. The critical value for the z test is based on a two-tailed test and an α level selected by the researcher.

If the obtained z score is greater than ±1.96, the researcher would reject the null hypothesis and accept the alternative. The conclusion would be that there is a significant difference in the ranks when comparing the two groups.

HYPOTHESIS CONSTRUCTION

The following hypotheses are tested using the Wilcoxon rank-sum test:

Null Hypothesis: The sum of the ranks for the two groups is equal.
Alternative Hypothesis: The sum of the ranks for the two groups is not equal.

Because the data are ordinal and one wishes to determine whether there are significant differences in the ranks between groups, the Wilcoxon rank-sum test is appropriate.

TEST FORMULA

The following formula is used to calculate the Wilcoxon rank sum (Kuzma 1992, 218–20):

$$\text{Expected Rank} = \frac{n_1(n_1+n_2+1)}{2}$$

$$\text{Standard Error} = \frac{n_1 n_2 (n_1 + n_2 + 1)}{12}$$

$$z \text{ Test} = \frac{\text{Observed Rank in Group 1 - Expected Rank}}{\text{Standard Error}}$$

SAMPLE PROBLEM

Twenty subjects were ranked according to the number of lost days on the job, then grouped by treatment clinic. The safety manager wishes to determine if there is a significant difference in observed ranks for the number of days to recover on the basis of the clinic.

The following table was developed:

Subject	Days to Recover	Clinic	Overall Ranking
1	15	B	16
2	30	B	19.5
3	26	B	17
4	27	B	18
5	3	B	4.5
6	2	A	1.5
7	4	A	6
8	5	A	7
9	3	A	4.5
10	1	A	1
11	2	B	1.5
12	7	A	9
13	8	A	10
14	9	A	11
15	12	B	13.5
16	30	B	19.5
17	11	A	12
18	14	B	15
19	6	A	8
20	12	B	13.5

For tied rankings, the ranks that the numbers will occupy are added, and then divided by the number of ties. For example, if the first two lowest numbers were the same, they would use rank values 1 and 2, and the total of 3. Each value would receive a rank of 1.5 (3/2). The ranking would continue with 3, 4, and so on.

In the next step, the rankings for the two groups are rearranged by group.

Subject	Days to Recover	Clinic	Overall Ranking
B	16	A	1.5
B	19.5	A	6
B	17	A	7
B	18	A	4.5
B	4.5	A	1
B	13.5	A	9
B	19.5	A	10
B	1.5	A	11
B	15	A	12
B	13.5	A	8
Total Ranks	138		70
Average Ranks	13.8		7

Step 1: Hypothesis construction

Null Hypothesis: The sum of the ranks for the two groups is equal.
Alternative Hypothesis: The sum of the ranks for the two groups is not equal.

Step 2: Statistical test

Because the data are ordinal in nature and we are dealing with two groups, the Wilcoxon rank-sum test is the appropriate statistical test.

Step 3: Determine the critical value

The researcher selected an α level of .05; therefore, using the normal distribution and a two-tailed test, the critical score is ±1.96. The decision rule would be to reject the null hypothesis and accept the alternative hypothesis if the obtained z value is greater than the critical value of ±1.96.

Step 4: Calculate the Wilcoxon rank sum

To calculate the Wilcoxon rank sum, the researcher must first determine the sum of the ranks for the two groups. The sum of the ranks and the average ranks appear in the previous data table. Next, the expected rank and standard error is calculated for the data as follows and the observed rank is statistically compared to the expected rank:

$$\text{Expected Rank} = \frac{10(10 + 10 + 1)}{2} = 105$$

$$\text{Standard Error} = \sqrt{\frac{(10)(10)(21)}{12}} = 13.23$$

$$z \text{ Test} = \frac{138 - 105}{13.23} = 2.50$$

Step 5: Decision rule

The obtained z value of 2.50 is greater than ±1.96; therefore, the null hypothesis is rejected and the alternative is accepted. The researcher concludes that the observed ranks for the groups are significantly different from what was expected.

Cochran's Q Test

Cochran's Q test is used to determine rankings over a series of items for a given population.

TEST ASSUMPTIONS

The assumptions are that, first, with the items being ranked, there are only two possible outcomes for each item, such as yes/no or pass/fail. Second, subjects in the population are considered repeated measures, meaning that each subject is evaluated on the array of items.

HYPOTHESIS CONSTRUCTION

Null Hypothesis: The probability of success is constant over all treatments.
Alternative Hypothesis: The probability of success is not constant over all treatments.

TEST FORMULA

If the data are categorical, with two possible outcomes, and each subject is repeatedly measured, Cochran's Q test can be used. The formula used to calculate Cochran's Q is as follows (Hays 1988, 820–22):

$$Q = \frac{J(J-1) \, \Sigma(Y_j - \overline{T})^2}{[J(\Sigma Y_k)] - (\Sigma Y_k^2)}$$

$$df = J - 1$$

Where:

$\overline{T}$ Average of the column totals
ΣY_k Sum of the rows
Y_j Sum of the columns
J Number of groups
ΣY_k^2 Sum of the squared row totals

To calculate Cochran's Q, the researcher must create a data table of the outcomes for each case across all measures. A 1 or a 0 is recorded for each trial. Then the results are summed for each case. For each trial, the results are summed for all cases, and the overall average rank is computed for all cases and all trials. Lastly, the case results are squared, then summed for all cases.

Cochran's Q follows a χ^2 distribution with $(J - 1)$ degrees of freedom. The obtained Cochran's Q is compared to the critical value.

If Cochran's Q is greater than the critical value, the null hypothesis is rejected and the alternative accepted. The researcher may conclude that the distribution of 1s is not uniform across the groups.

SAMPLE PROBLEM

Step 1: Hypothesis construction

Null Hypothesis: The probability of success is constant over all treatments.
Alternative Hypothesis: The probability of success is not constant over all treatments.

Step 2: Statistical test
Because the data are categorical, with two possible outcomes, and each subject is repeatedly measured, Cochran's Q test can be used.
Step 3: Calculate Cochran's Q
To calculate Cochran's Q, the researcher must establish a data table of the outcomes for each case across all measures. A 1 or a 0 is recorded for each trial. Then the results are summed for each case. For each trial, the results are summed for all cases and the overall average rank is computed for all cases and all trials. Lastly, the case results are squared, then summed for all cases. The data for the sample problem are presented below:

Case	Trial 1	Trial 2	Trial 3	Total y_k	y^2
1	1	1	0	2	4
2	1	0	1	2	4
3	0	1	1	2	4
4	0	1	0	1	1
5	1	1	0	2	4
6	1	0	1	2	4
7	0	0	0	0	0
8	1	1	1	3	9
9	0	0	0	0	0
10	1	0	0	1	1
Total y_j	6	5	4	15	31

To calculate Cochran's Q, the values for the variables in the formula are as follows:

Number of groups	=	3
Average of the column totals	=	15/3 = 5
Sum of the squared row totals	=	31

To calculate Cochran's Q, the values for the variables are placed in the formula as follows:

$$Q = \frac{3(3\text{-}1)[(6\text{-}5)^2 + (5\text{-}5)^2 + (4\text{-}5)^2]}{[(3)(15)] - (31)} = .86$$

$$df = 3 - 1 = 2$$

Step 4: Determine significance
Cochran's Q follows a χ^2 distribution with 2 degrees of freedom. The critical value is 5.99 for 2 degrees of freedom and an α level of .05. Because the obtained Cochran's Q is not greater than the critical value, the null hypothesis is not rejected. The researcher may conclude that the distribution of 1s is not uniform across the groups.

Chapter Summary

Nonparametric statistics are used to analyze data that are not assumed to follow a known distribution. An example of data that requires the use of nonparametric statistics is frequency data and rank data. There are numerous statistical tests and procedures available to the researcher to analyze these forms of distribution-free data. The most commonly used tests are the χ^2 test for association and χ^2 test for goodness of fit. Both can be used with frequency data and they can both use the χ^2 distribution.

Chapter Review Exercises

1. Define nonparametric statistics.
2. Describe the data requirements for nonparametric statistics.
3. Describe the process one would follow when using the χ^2 test of independence.
4. Describe the process one would follow when using the Wilcoxon rank-sum test.
5. Describe the process one would follow when using the χ^2 goodness of fit test.
6. What are the data requirements for the χ^2 goodness of fit test?
7. What statistical test is used to test for a significant Wilcoxon rank-sum?
8. What hypothesis is tested to determine significance in a Wilcoxon rank-sum test?
9. How would one adjust for ties in the Wilcoxon rank-sum test procedure?
10. What is the critical score for a χ^2 test with 15 degrees of freedom and an α level of .05?
11. How would one calculate the degrees of freedom for a χ^2 test that uses a 4 × 3 table?
12. A safety manager collected data from 50 employees that used back belts as a regular part of their job. She asked them if they felt the back belt fit properly, which they responded to as yes or no. She then broke the sample down into three departments. The data collected were as follows:

Back Belt Fit Properly	Department A	Department B	Department C
Yes	12	8	14
No	8	11	16

What conclusions can be drawn?

13. A company had five different types of safety glasses for employees to choose from. Assuming there is an equal chance for an employee to choose any of the five types, what conclusions can the safety manager reach on the basis of 50 employees' selection of glasses as shown in the table below?

Glasses	Selected
Type 1	13
Type 2	8
Type 3	7
Type 4	15
Type 5	7

CHAPTER 9

Survey Research

Survey research is a systematic method for obtaining information from a population. When properly designed and implemented, survey research provides valid and reliable results. There are guidelines that one should follow when designing and implementing a survey study. These rules range from proper selection of the target population, to the design of the instrument, to the statistical calculations. When properly conducted, the survey research should be reproducible, representative of the population (making it generalizable), and free from bias.

Types of Survey Studies

Survey studies can be classified into two broad categories: experimental studies and descriptive or observational studies. In an experimental study, there is one experimental group that is compared to a control group. Descriptive studies include cross-section studies, cohort studies, and case–control studies. Cross-section studies break a population into groups and examine the population at a specific point in time. Cohort studies examine a population over a period of time. In case-control studies, the population is examined retrospectively and comparisons are made between those exposed and those not exposed.

Planning a Survey Study

COLLECTION AND MAINTENANCE

When collecting data, it is important to maintain and organize the data in a manner that removes possibilities for error. The researcher should first establish the list of variables that are going to be examined. The variables should only include those characteristics the researcher is concerned about. Next, the method in which the variables will be measured should be established. The next step is to develop a code sheet for the variables. For each variable, the available values and their assigned labels are established. The data are then arranged in a spreadsheet format, with the variables listed across the top and the cases going down. Using this technique will decrease data entry and analysis errors. The data entry is then performed using the information off the sheet.

Outline for Planning a Survey

In any research study, careful planning in the beginning helps avoid problems in the analysis phase. Early in the planning stages, the researcher should develop specific questions that need to be answered. The type of data needed to answer the questions should be determined in conjunction with the statistical procedure. Survey research studies fall apart when the survey instrument does not ask the appropriate questions required to obtain usable data, or when the format of the data obtained cannot be analyzed using the necessary statistical procedure. Another common problem with survey research is that the researcher compiles a survey instrument, collects the data, and then tries to determine how they should be analyzed. Pilot testing can also be used to alleviate the problems with the survey items. Problems pilot testing can identify include poorly worded items, confusing directions, and improper item formats.

A recommended process that should be followed when conducting survey research is as follows (Backstrom and Hursh-Cesar 1981, 24):

1. Make a written statement of the purpose of the survey.
2. Write out the objectives and hypotheses.
3. Specify the target population.
4. List the variables to be measured.
5. Review existing pertinent data.
6. Outline the methods of data collection.
7. Establish the time frame.
8. Design the questionnaire.
9. Pretest the questionnaire.
10. Select subjects for the sample.
11. Collect the data.
12. Edit, code, and enter the data on a computer.
13. Analyze the data.
14. Report the findings

Step 1: Make a written statement of the purpose of the survey.
The purpose of the survey should be well thought out, carefully defined, and clearly stated in two or three sentences. This step will assist in carrying out the subsequent steps. Without it, a survey is doomed to fail.
Step 2: Formulate objectives and hypotheses.
A descriptive survey seeks to estimate one or more characteristics of a population. That, quite simply, is its specific objective. An analytical survey seeks to examine rela-

tionships among some specified characteristics. To carry it out, one needs to define the hypotheses to be tested.

Step 3: Specify the target population.

The target population is the group of people from whom inferences are to be drawn. This population may well be restricted to one from which the investigator may feasibly draw a sample. To test the research hypothesis, it is essential to estimate certain essential characteristics of individual members of the target population. In statistical sampling, a member of a population is often referred to as an element. It may be a person, a mother–child pair, or some local group of persons such as a household. Measurements are taken on the element. The population can be defined as the collection of all elements.

Step 4: List the variables.

Once the target population is defined and elements are identified, list the variables that are to be assessed on each element. For example, a target population might be all the students enrolled in a college course who have successfully stopped smoking during the last 12 months. The element would be each member of the class possessing that characteristic. Variables measured might be age, sex, amount of smoking, and number of years of smoking before quitting.

There is an endless list of potential variables that can be generated using a survey instrument. The key is to only include those items that are pertinent to the questions the researcher wishes to answer. All variables should be clearly defined during the planning stages.

Step 5: Review existing data.

It is important to review current literature on the topic being surveyed so that one can determine the current hypotheses that are regarded as pertinent. It is often advisable to use standardized questions to aid in demonstrating the validity and reliability of the instrument.

Step 6: Decide how to collect data.

There are numerous methods available for collecting data, and each has certain advantages and disadvantages. Factors to consider include the amount of time the researcher has to conduct the study, the costs associated with the study, and the ability to obtain the data. For example, the interview process is considered more costly than mail surveys, but interviews may provide more in-depth information. Response rates are also important in designing the method for collecting the data. Mail surveys may have low response rates, especially if they are being sent to the general public.

Step 7: Establish the time frame.

It is necessary to establish a realistic time frame for the schedule of survey events. The schedule should not be so tight that succeeding steps are jeopardized if there is a delay in preceding events. Plan for backup procedures and personnel to avoid delays.

Step 8: Design the survey questionnaire.

Questions need to be carefully worded so as not to confuse the respondent or arouse extraneous attitudes. The questions should provide a clear understanding of the information sought. Avoid ambiguity and wording that may be perceived as a way to elicit a specific response. Questions may be open ended, multiple choice, completion, or a variation of these. One should avoid overly complex questions.

The essential principles to keep in mind while constructing a questionnaire are that it should (l) be easy for the respondent to read, understand, and answer; (2) motivate the respondent to answer; (3) be designed for efficient data processing; (4) have a well-designed professional appearance; and (5) be designed to minimize missing data.

Step 9: Pretest the questionnaire.

It is not possible to anticipate in advance all the potential problems that may occur when one administers a questionnaire, so it is important to pretest it. A pretest will identify questions that respondents tend to misinterpret, omit, or answer inappropriately. The pretest should be done on a handful of individuals similar to but not included in the target population and should use the same methodology that will be used in the actual survey.

Step 10: Select the sample.

One should select the sample in such a manner that valid statistical inferences can be drawn regarding the target population. One should obtain a representative sample that minimizes sampling bias and is designed for economy of operation. Sampling designs include simple random, systematic random, stratified random, and multistage sampling.

Step 11: Collect the data.

Collect the data to maximize the responses with a completed and pretested questionnaire. This step requires careful planning and supervision to ensure data of good quality. One should attain the following objectives: (1) maximize the response rate by minimizing nonresponses, (2) keep track of the nonrespondents, (3) obtain some information on non-respondents, (4) avoid duplication, (5) avoid failing to contact part of the sample, (6) protect confidentiality of the data, (7) ensure anonymity, and (8) maintain a cooperative spirit. Also, interviewers should be well trained and coached regarding how to approach the respondents, how to conduct the interview, how to handle various answers, and how to inform respondents about what is expected of them during the interview.

Step 12: Edit and code the data.

Editing data is analogous to editing a newspaper to make sure that the text meets certain standards and that errors are corrected. The editor checks for missing data, inconsistencies, and other problems that can be remedied. Editing of data should be done as soon as possible after data collection.

To permit computerized analysis of data, it is essential that the variables be reduced to a form in which a numerical value may be assigned to each possible choice. This process is referred to as coding. It is carried out simultaneously with editing. Coding may be done either by use of an ad hoc coding system specifically developed for the database or by use of a standard coding system.

The current method of choice is to enter data directly via an interactive terminal. In this way, a validation program is able to inform the key-entry operator immediately about possibly invalid data. To maintain accuracy, it is essential that, by program or otherwise, the data entry be verified.

Step 13: Analyze the data.

After the data have been collected, edited, coded, and key-entered, it is almost ready for analysis. But a preliminary step—some advance data analysis to ferret out possible outliers—is needed. Look at the distribution of the various variables. Provide an item analysis for the variables of special interest and assess the amount of missing data. Once this analysis is completed, one should be ready to perform the major data analysis, a task dictated by the specific objectives of the survey.

Step 14: Report the findings.

The report should begin with background information that provides a rationale for the study. It should indicate the specific objectives that the survey seeks to accomplish. A methods section should describe the target population, the test instruments, and the sampling design. The results section should discuss the findings and possible future implications.

Constructing the Instrument

One of the first places survey research studies fail to obtain satisfactory statistical results is in the design of the survey instrument. Careful planning must be done in developing the instrument to ensure that items will obtain the information needed and that the information will answer the research questions.

When developing the survey instrument, some essential points to remember about item development are that (Beckstrom and Hursh-Cesar 1981, 34):

- The item should measure something that is relevant to the problem.
- There should be agreement on the meaning of the question.
- There should be agreement on the understanding of the item.
- All possible categories should be represented.
- Numbers can be assigned to the responses.
- Questions and responses have no wording problems.
- The questions and answers are in a format that keypunchers can master.
- The items survive a pretest.

Types of Survey Items

Survey items can be classified into groups based on the information sought from the respondents. Fact questions try to obtain information about the subject. Examples of fact questions include various demographic questions such as age, gender, and date of birth.

Opinion and attitude questions try to obtain information that is subjective in nature. These questions try to elicit information about a person's feelings, beliefs, ideas, and values. Information obtained from these types of items can change from time to time depending on the person and the nature of the questions.

Informational items attempt to obtain information about a situation that is based on the respondent's knowledge of that event. For example, when a safety manager obtains information from a person about an accident, he is relying on the person's knowledge of the event. The data collected from a person that directly witnessed the accident may be quite different compared with that from a person who only heard about it.

Forms of Questions

Selecting the form of the question is very important in survey research design. It is the form of the question that will determine the type of information obtained and the format of the data collected. There are two major categories of question forms: unstructured and structured questions (Beckstrom and Hursh-Cesar 1981, 128).

UNSTRUCTURED QUESTIONS

Unstructured questions are free-response or open-ended questions. These types of questions allow the respondent to provide answers in their own words, to the level they choose and in the way that they choose. An example of an open-ended question would be "What was the cause of the accident?" The person completing the survey can provide as little or as much detail as he or she chooses. One person may talk about the sequence of events, while another person may respond with two words.

Open-ended questions typically are used when the researcher is not sure of the range of responses that may be obtained or he has limited knowledge as to the potential responses. Responses from open-ended questions may be analyzed and later categorized by the researcher for analysis. It is impossible to quantitatively analyze responses from open-ended items in their original state without recoding the information. Another downside for open-ended questions is the amount of time they take to answer and the amount of space needed on a survey form to complete the item. It takes far less space and time to answer items that require a person to check categories or circle numbers on a scale.

STRUCTURED QUESTIONS

A structured question is one that gives fixed-response alternatives (Backstrom and Hursh-Cesar 1981, 130). Examples of fixed-response items include Likert-type scales, where a person has to circle a value on the scale, check a box from a set of items, or rank items.

Dichotomous items provide the respondent with two options from which to choose. Examples of dichotomous items include yes/no items and good/bad items. Multiple-choice items allow the respondent to choose from several alternatives. Related to the form of the item is the format of the data collected. In one item, the responses may be considered categorical, whereas in another they may be ordinal. It is imperative that the researcher know the format of the data that will be obtained from a particular item early in the survey design phase. This is to ensure that there are statistical procedures available to analyze the data and answer the questions the researcher chooses to answer.

Within the fixed-response form of questions, the data collected from the items can be nominal, ordinal, interval, or ratio. Nominal data, otherwise referred to as categorical, provide the respondent with mutually exclusive choices. An example of a nominal item would be to select the box that describes the person's place of ethnic origin. Nominal responses cannot be mathematically compared. They cannot be added or subtracted, and no category is bigger or smaller than another.

Ordinal items yield data that are ordered or ranked in some manner. A person can take ordinal responses and rank them from lowest to highest. The differences in the rankings signify differences in the construct being measured.

Paired comparisons are another type of ranking measure. In these types of data, the subject is asked to compare A versus B, B versus C, etc. A weakness of ordinal measures is that there is no magnitude between the rankings. A difference between a rank of 1 and 2 is the same as the difference between the rank of 3 and 4. We can only say 2 is greater than 1, but not by how much.

Interval data, in contrast, indicates distances between values. Numerically equal intervals represent equal degrees or distances along a continuum of measurement. A common interval scale is degrees on a thermometer. Such measures show both order and distance between any points on the scale. It is the same distance between any points on the scale. Therefore, values on the scale can be added and subtracted. On an interval scale, zero is a placeholder.

Ratio data, on the other hand, do not have zero as a placeholder. The value zero represents the absence of the characteristic. Values on the ratio scale have magnitude. Magnitude means that we can say something is twice as heavy, three times taller, etc. We cannot make these comparisons with things measured on any other scale, including the interval scale. For example, something that is 0 pounds really does not have any weight. Contrast this to "0 degrees" on the Fahrenheit scale, which gives the item measured a temperature.

Rating Scales

Scaled responses are alternative answers, each having a different weight attached to it. The weight is a measure of psychological distance (intensity) between each response. Rating scales present respondents with words or phrases and ask them to indicate the extent to which they describe their feelings. There are several variations in rating scales.

Likert-type scales

When developing a Likert-type scale, there are limits to how meaningful the categories can be (Beckstrom and Hursh-Cesar 1981, 135–38). In other words, if too few categories are provided, then the information is meaningless to the researcher. An example of this is when three categories are provided on the scale and everyone selects one category. On the other hand, if the scale is being used for a telephone interview and there are ten different categories, the process of completing the interview is bogged down because the respondents must be continually reminded of the various values. Generally speaking, a Likert-type scale of five to seven items is probably as many categories as most respondents can use meaningfully for most rating tasks.

When placing a scale on a survey instrument, the item the respondent is to answer should be clearly stated. The possible responses in the continua should correspond to the item. One should avoid asking a yes/no-type question and then asking the person to respond on a scale format. Each point on the scale should be labeled with the most positive response to the left of the scale and the most negative to the right. The ends of the scales should be opposites, with the center being neutral. Odd-numbered scales fit this model most favorably. The Likert-type scale, for example, presents five or sometimes six degrees of possible agreement. An example of a Likert-type scale is

1	2	3	4	5
Disagree Strongly	Disagree Moderately	Neutral	Agree Moderately	Agree Strongly

To develop a Likert-type scale, some common things to remember include the following (Beckstrom and Hursh-Cesar 1981, 135–37):

• Use an odd number of categories, preferably 5.
• The labels for the ends of the scale should be exact opposites.
• The center-point should be neutral.
• Do not mix and match various scales within a survey.
• Provide a label for each point on the scale, and label each scale.
• Provide directions at the beginning of the Likert-scale activities.

Semantic Differential Scales

Semantic differential scales are seven-step rating scales anchored by opposite objectives (Beckstrom and Hursh-Cesar 1981, 136). The respondent is asked to indicate his or her feelings toward the item by selecting a number 1 through 7 on the scale. Notice that only the ends are labeled in a semantic differential scale.

Bad							Good
	1	2	3	4	5	6	7	

Formatting Questionnaires for the Mail

One of the most commonly used tools to collect data for research studies is the mail survey. The guidelines a researcher should follow when developing a mail survey can improve the data collection and the response rates from the subjects. A general rule of thumb for mail surveys is to keep the instrument simple and only have the respondent provide answers to items that are of importance to the research study at hand. Some general points to keep in mind when developing a mail survey are as follows (Beckstrom and Hursh-Cesar 1981, 232):

- **White Space:** Use space liberally. Do not clutter pages with unnecessary information that the respondent does not need to answer the questions.
- **Identification:** Use an identification number that identifies the intended respondent.
- **Physical Form:** Make the print large enough to be read by weak or failing eyes. Print black on white or black on pale yellow for best readability. If the budget permits it, use a distinctive-colored letterhead and/or typeface to give it greater authority.
- **Language:** If there is reason to expect mailing to non-English-speaking respondents, print a bilingual version of the questionnaire as well.
- **Length:** Keep the questionnaire short. Respondents must believe they can complete it on the spot without significant effort or undue time. For a population survey, a format of one page front and back is ideal. If it has to be longer, it should be in a brochure.
- **Simplicity:** Almost none of the design techniques of telephone surveys can be used in mail questionnaires that are used by trained interviewers. Do not use respondent-selection keys or complicated schematics. Keep it simple, proceeding from one question to the next.
- **No Variation:** Unless truly unavoidable, do not use filter questions. Instruct respondents to answer all questions. Do not make them responsible for determining their eligibility to answer questions.
- **Spacing:** Physical layout determines the ease with which a person gets through a questionnaire. Careful attention to the spatial arrangement includes ensuring that the information is not crowded on the page.
- **Consistency:** The format of the instrument should be consistent. The items should be arranged in a similar format using the same indentation and alignment so that items are in the same location on each page.

Sound Survey Research Procedures

When conducting the survey study, there are many guidelines one can follow to ensure that the survey research is successful. Some major characteristics of survey research design include the following:

MEASURABLE OBJECTIVE

The survey should be developed using measurable objectives, and the survey instrument should have a sound design that incorporates statistical analysis.

REPRESENTATIVE POPULATION

The population that is selected must be representative of that from which a response is desired. For example, it would not make sense to try to determine the perceptions of a population of males aged 30 to 55 but administer the survey instrument to females. While this would seem absurd, research is often conducted with a sample that is not representative of the population and, therefore, the results are not valid.

MATCH THE HYPOTHESIS TO THE STATISTICAL TESTS

When the study is designed, the instruments, the objective of the study, and the statistical methods that will be used must be identified before the survey instrument is developed. Many times, the overall question is formulated, but the items asked on the instrument do not answer the questions the researcher has. Another problem may be that the formats of the questions do not lend themselves to a statistical procedure that can test the hypotheses. For example, a researcher wishes to determine if there is a significant difference in the average ages of the respondents on the basis of their gender. An appropriate statistical test that could be used to answer this question is the z test for means. However, if the researcher forms the question designed to obtain the respondent's age as a categorical question, then the z test cannot be used, and as a result, the hypothesis cannot be tested.

CONDUCT BACKGROUND RESEARCH

The process for designing an effective survey instrument is to perform background investigation into the problem. By reviewing past research, the researcher can use the information to develop credible hypotheses that can be tested. The hypothesis the researcher develops ties the statistical procedures to the format of the questions.

INSTRUMENT VALIDITY AND RELIABILITY

Two important characteristics of the overall survey instrument are its validity and reliability.

The validity of the survey instrument refers to whether the questions are asking what the researcher thinks they are asking and whether the respondent is reading, interpreting, and answering the items in the manner in which the researcher believes. There are a number of ways that validity of a survey instrument can be ascertained. Some of the more common methods are to pilot test the instrument with a second instrument that has already been determined to be valid. The assumption therefore is that if the respondents answer in the same manner on both instruments, then it can be assumed that the new item is measuring the same construct that the proven item is.

A statistical procedure for determining validity of the survey instrument is the correlation coefficient. By running a bivariate correlation between like items on different forms, one may deduce that the items are measuring the same content. An alternate method for confirming validity of an instrument is through the use of subject matter experts. The experts, by their knowledge of the field and of the items being asked, can make an educated validation of the content of the items.

The reliability of an instrument refers to the consistency in manner in which people are responding to the survey items. Reliability must be confirmed before validity can be confirmed. In other words, an instrument cannot be valid if it is not reliable. On the other hand, just because an instrument has been found to be reliable does not necessarily mean that it is valid. A method for determining reliability includes administering alternate forms of the instrument to the same people over a period during a pilot test. If the people respond to the items in the same manner, then the instrument may be considered reliable. If there are significant differences in the manner in which a person answered the items during the first round and the second, then further study needs to be conducted to determine the reason for these differences. There are a number of statistical procedures available to determine reliability. They include correlations between rounds for each item and specific statistical techniques designed to determine the reliability of an instrument.

COVER LETTERS AND INSTRUCTIONS

Once the target population and the questions that one wishes to answer using the survey instrument have been identified, the survey instrument must be arranged. There are a variety of different planning and organization guidelines to follow when developing the survey instrument. In a cover letter to the potential respondents (or at the top of the survey instrument), the purpose of the survey should be described. The cover letter should name the organization that is conducting the survey and the purpose of the study. There should be overall instructions to the respondents provided, including what time frame they have to respond to the survey and how they send it back, and so on. The instructions should also include a statement about confidentiality. If the respondents are volunteers for the survey, it should be stated. Not only should the letter inform the respondents that individual surveys will not be published, but also that the results will be published in a manner in which it will not be possible for individuals to be identified. If the respondents cannot be identified by the instrument, this should be stated. The respondents should also be given the chance to obtain copies of the results after they are compiled.

Each of the various tasks should have directions, no matter how simple it may appear to be to complete the instrument. If only one response in a section is desired, this should be stated. If a person may check more than one item, this should also be stated.

SAMPLING FOR SURVEYS

A variety of sampling methods have previously been presented. These methods include simple random samples, cluster samples, and systematic random samples. The key to making the results generalizable to the larger population is to ensure that the population selected is representative of the overall population and that the selection is free from bias.

CALCULATING SAMPLE SIZES

To calculate the sample size for a survey study, the researcher must determine what the probability of detecting a significant difference is (if one actually exists), or otherwise stated, what the power of the test statistic being used is. This is the probability of correctly rejecting the null hypothesis when the null hypothesis is false, that is, the probability of not committing a Type II error. Varieties of formulas can be used to calculate sample sizes, depending on the statistical test being used. In correlation studies, there are power tables with which the researcher with a determined power level and an anticipated correlation coefficient can determine how many subjects must be selected to achieve that power level. As the power level increases, the number of subjects required in the study increases. A researcher can reach a point on the power tables where significant increases in the number of subjects are required for only minimal returns in improvement in the power levels.

SURVEY RESEARCH LIMITATIONS

There are limitations to survey research, one of which is the fact that they can become costly to conduct. The numbers of subjects may be extremely large, which will increase costs as well as time considerations. For those wanting relatively fast responses to a particular problem, the survey method may be time consuming. The first phase of the study requires that a pilot test be conducted and that the respondents be given a sufficient length of time to respond to the survey. The data inputting can take considerable time, as well as the analysis.

PILOT TESTING

A pilot test is crucial for successful survey research. By pilot testing a survey, the researchers take what they perceive as a good product and administer it to a group of subjects who will be representative of those participating in the actual study. The subjects in the pilot test should not be included in the actual study. There are biases introduced when people are asked to respond to the same instrument multiple times.

In the pilot study, the researcher is looking for problems that may occur in the administration and evaluation of the survey results. This is the point where the researcher may find that not all possible choices are provided on the survey, or respondents have not understood the tasks they are asked to complete, are completing sections of the survey incorrectly, or are writing in comments on the form. This is also where the researcher may find that the format of the items does not lend itself well to a particular statistical procedure.

Modifications should be made to the instrument, based on the results of the pilot study, before it is sent out on a large scale. If major modifications are made to the instrument, it may require another pilot testing before it is ready to go out to the study sample.

PERMISSION TO USE HUMAN SUBJECTS

In various organizations, conducting research on human subjects requires permission from a review board. The purpose of the review is to ensure that confidentiality is being maintained and that no adverse effects from such research will occur. The process usually requires that the researcher submit the research plans and controls that will be in place to ensure that subjects are being treated ethically. The approval is required before any studies can be conducted.

Chapter Summary

Survey research is a very useful and widely used method for obtaining information about a population. It requires proper planning and execution to ensure that the results are representative and free from bias. The survey process includes proper identification of the population from which to draw the sample, development of a sound survey instrument, and proper analysis of the results. The survey instrument format and the items contained within should follow generally recognized formats to ensure valid and reliable results.

Chapter Review Exercises

A safety manager put together a survey instrument for a training program. For the following survey items, describe the potential problems and formatting errors that should be addressed before they are used in an instrument.

1. What is your age? _____ 15–20   _____ 20–25   _____ 25–30
2. Did you complete the training program or must you still enroll? _____ Yes   _____ No
3. What is your overall impression of the program? _____ Good   _____ Bad
4. On a scale of 1 to 5, how would you rate the content? 1 2 3 4 5
5. Using the scale below, please rate your overall satisfaction with the training program.

1	2	3	4	5
Disagree Strongly	Disagree Moderately	Neutral	Agree Moderately	Agree Strongly

6. Using the scale below, please rate your agreement with the following statement: This training program was useful.

1	2	3	4	5
Disagree Strongly	Disagree Moderately	Neutral	Agree Moderately	Agree Strongly

7. Using the scale below, please rate your agreement with the following statement: I will recommend this course to others.

Bad   Good

     1   2   3   4   5   6   7

8. Describe three major points to provide in a cover letter or at the top of the survey instrument.
9. What are some benefits of using structured items?
10. What does pilot testing do for survey research?

CHAPTER 10

Experimental Design

Experimental Design Uses

In Chapter 9, the one-way ANOVA was presented as a method for determining if there are significant differences in the average measures for a sample by groups. The ANOVA procedure can be expanded to a variety of more complex procedures in which the subjects may be randomly assigned to groups, referred to as treatments. The number of treatments can be quite numerous, and the measures taken within each treatment can be single or repeated.

The term *experimental design* refers to the plan that is used for assigning experimental conditions to subjects and the statistical analysis associated with the plan (Kirk 1982, 1). An experiment, by definition, involves the manipulation of one or more variables by an experimenter to determine the effect of this manipulation on another variable. By following a set of experimental design guidelines, the researcher can statistically design an experiment that can test hypotheses and control for various effects that can influence it. The purpose of this chapter is to introduce the researcher to a few of the more common experimental design methods and provide a summary of the steps a researcher performs when using these designs. Actually performing the studies requires considerable preparation in statistics and research methods.

Research Hypotheses and Experimental Design

The design of an experiment to investigate a scientific or research hypothesis involves a number of interrelated activities (Kirk 1982, 3):

1. Formulation of statistical hypotheses that are germane to the scientific hypothesis. A statistical hypothesis is a statement about one or more parameters of a population. Statistical hypotheses are rarely identical to scientific hypotheses, but are testable formulations of scientific hypotheses.

2. Determination of the experimental conditions (independent variables) to be employed and the extraneous conditions (nuisance variables) that must be controlled.
3. Specification of the number of experimental units (subjects) required and the population from which they are to be sampled.
4. Specification of the procedure for assigning the experimental conditions to the subjects.
5. Determination of the measurement to be recorded (dependent variable) for each subject and the statistical analyses that will be performed.

Dependent and Independent Variables

The first step in any experiment is to identify the variables to measure. The choice of an appropriate dependent variable may be based on theoretical considerations, although in many investigations the choice is determined by practical considerations. If it is necessary to evaluate two or more dependent variables simultaneously, a multivariate ANOVA design can be used. The selection of the most fruitful variables to measure should be determined by a consideration of the sensitivity, reliability, distribution, and practicality of the possible dependent variables (Kirk 1982, 4). From previous experience, an experimenter may know that one dependent variable is more sensitive than another to the effects of a treatment or that one dependent variable is more reliable, that is, gives more consistent results, than another variable. Choosing a dependent variable that possesses these two characteristics may minimize the amount of time and effort required to investigate a research hypothesis (Kirk 1982, 4). Another important consideration in selecting a dependent variable is whether the observations within each treatment level (or combination of treatment levels in the case of multi-treatment experiments) would be approximately normally distributed (Kirk 1982, 4).

Types of Experimental Designs

There are various experimental designs that are commonly used in research studies. Although this book will not present the math required to perform the procedures, this section should give the researcher an idea as to the process that is followed when such studies are performed. All of the procedures can be performed using some of the more sophisticated statistical computer software. They all also use the F ratio to determine statistical significance in the same manner as the ANOVA.

ONE-WAY ANOVA

The one-way ANOVA procedure presented in the previous chapter uses one independent variable and one dependent variable. The independent variable is the grouping variable to which subjects are randomly assigned or belong. The dependent variable is the continuous variable measured once for each subject in the sample. The assumption of this experimental design is that a statistically significant F ratio implies that the differences in the dependent variables are due to group membership.

COMPLETELY RANDOMIZED DESIGN

In a completely randomized block design, subjects are randomly assigned to the various treatments in an experiment. This is considered the simplest form of an experimental design. There are no characteristics that the subjects are matched by prior to the experiment. The subjects are randomly selected, then randomly assigned to each level of the treatment. The only restriction in the assignment may be that subjects are assigned so that there are the same number in each treatment level.

RANDOMIZED BLOCK DESIGN

In a randomized block design, the subjects in the experiment are grouped according to a particular characteristic. This grouping, or "blocking" technique, is used to reduce the effects that the blocking characteristic may have on the overall results of the study (Kirk 1982, 12–13). For example, assume that a researcher wishes to examine the effects a new drug has on a particular disease. It is reasonably assumed by the researcher prior to the experiment that the length of time a person has the disease prior to treatment has an effect on the length of time it takes for the drug to eliminate the symptoms. To control for this phenomenon, subjects are first grouped according to the length of time they had the disease prior to treatment. Then subjects in the blocks are randomly assigned a treatment drug and the results are evaluated. By blocking subjects first and then making comparisons, the effects of the length of time with the disease prior to treatment are controlled and the results should give a true indication of the drug's effectiveness.

LATIN SQUARE DESIGN

In a Latin square design, more than one nuisance variable can be controlled in the experiment (Kirk 1982, 14). In the completely randomized block design, the subjects were first grouped according to the length of time with a disease prior to treatment. A Latin square design allows the researcher to group subjects according to a second variable as well. Let's take the previous example, but instead of just having length of time as an important factor, let's say that a second variable, age of the subject, is also important. To perform a Latin square design, the researcher groups subjects within each level of length of time and groups them according to age within each age category. One restriction for a Latin square design is that the number of groups for the first variable must equal the number of groups for the second blocking variable (Kirk 1982, 14–15). A second requirement is that the number of subjects in each block must be the same throughout all levels and all treatments (Kirk 1982, 14–15).

COMPLETELY RANDOMIZED FACTORIAL DESIGN

In this experimental design, subjects are randomly selected and assigned to groups in the experiment (Kirk 1982, 16–17). In a completely randomized factorial design, subjects are grouped by two or more variables. For example, assume that a safety manager wishes to determine if there are significant differences in the average number of days lost for repetitive motion injuries based on the type of training the subject received concerning the injury and the person that provided the training. To set up a completely randomized factorial design, subjects received training from one of three possible trainers using one of four possible training programs. The subjects were randomly assigned to the trainers and the trainers randomly selected the training program. To conduct this experiment, the researcher would statistically compare the average number of days lost for the various groups of subjects.

Chapter Summary

Experimental design is the process by which statistical comparisons can be made and hypotheses can be tested concerning means. There are varieties of experimental designs that can be used in research, many of which can be quite complex. This chapter introduced the reader to some of the more basic experimental designs and provided an understanding as to the comparisons that are being made and procedures used in assigning subjects to the treatment and control groups. Four common experimental designs presented were one-way ANOVA, completely randomized block design, randomized block design, and the Latin square design.

One-way ANOVA is the simplest of the experimental design procedures and uses one dependent variable and one independent variable. The more complex designs using Latin square, completely randomized block designs, and completely randomized factorial designs can have multiple independent variables as well as multiple measures for each subject. Each of these designs not only uses multiple treatment groups but also may assign members to treatment groups.

Chapter Review Exercises

1. What does the term *experimental design* mean?
2. Why is experimental design of importance to someone using literature concerning statistical research?

For each of the following experimental designs, summarize the process in conducting a study.

3. One-way ANOVA
4. Completely randomized block design

5. Randomized block design
6. Latin square design

For each of the following studies, what is the experimental design used?

7. A safety manager wanted to determine if there were significant differences in the average number of accidents reported each month for three different plants. Assuming that employment in any one of the three plants is random, what type of design should the manager use?

8. A safety manager wished to see if safety training could be used to reduce the average number of accidents in one plant. He randomly selected 30 employees and randomly assigned them to one of three different training programs. He then examined the average number of accidents reported for employees by training program attended.

9. The safety manager suspected that the length of employment with the company has an effect on accident involvement. To control for differences in tenure with the company, the manager first divided the employees into one of three groups for length of employment. Then he randomly assigned them to one of three training programs so that each training program had 10 subjects for each of the three length-of-employment categories. He then wanted to determine if the average numbers of accidents reported each month were significantly different from one another.

CHAPTER 11

Presenting Research

Data Presentation for Safety Professionals

As a regular part of their job, safety professionals are often required to communicate the results of their data analyses to others. This can range from summarizing the analyses in a written document to presenting the information in a meeting or presentation. Regardless of the format, there are guidelines one should follow when displaying and presenting the data.

Displaying Descriptive Statistics

Typically, descriptive statistics are summarized and displayed in a variety of formats. These include tables, charts, and graphs, to name a few. If the results are to be published, the formats for tables, graphs, and charts and applicable writing style may also be established by the journal. Some general guidelines to follow when developing tables, graphs, and charts are as follows (American Psychological Association 1995, 130–40):

- The number of main points should be limited in any one table, graph, or chart to that which can be easily understood.
- To clearly identify the material, a title that describes the content as to the subject, person, place, and time should always be included. Titles should be numbered.
- The body of the data must be arranged in a manner that is meaningful.
- The source of the information should always be identified, usually as a footnote.

DISPLAYING TABLES

A table is a set of data that is arranged in rows and columns. The purpose of a table is to present the frequency at which some event occurs in different categories or subdivisions of a variable. Some general guidelines for presenting data in tables are as follows:

- Tables should be simple. Two or three smaller tables are preferable to one large table.
- Tables should be self-explanatory.
- The title should be clear and concise. It should answer the question of what, when, and where.
- Each row and column should be labeled clearly and concisely. The specific units for the data measured should be given. If columns appear to run together, they should be separated with a vertical line.
- Row and column totals should be shown.
- Codes, abbreviations, or symbols should be explained in detail in a footnote.

Example Table

Table 1.   Smoking Habit by Gender[a]

	Smoker	Nonsmoker	Total
Male	15	25	40
Female	30	17	47
Total	45	42	87

[a]All cases from 1992 exit surveys.

BAR CHARTS

Bar charts provide a visual comparison of quantitative and categorical data. Two or more series of data with multiple categories can be presented on the same chart for comparison purposes (American Psychological Association 1995, 143). The chart is set up along two axes. The various categories are presented along the horizontal (x) axis. They may be arranged by frequency within a category, alphabetically, and so on. Bars are used to represent each of the categories. The vertical axis (y) represents the quantitative value of the observed variable defined on the x-axis. The y-axis begins at zero and continues to a point that includes all values that the bars represent. A cell on a bar chart is one group along the horizontal axis. A cell may have more than one bar. For example, assume that a researcher wishes to compare the frequency of accidents for three departments and within each department wishes to compare males to females. Along the horizontal axis there would be three cells, one representing each department. Within each cell, there would be two bars representing gender. A sample bar chart appears in Figure 11.1.

Some general guidelines to follow when constructing a bar chart are listed below:

- The vertical height of the bar represents the quantitative value of each variable/ category.

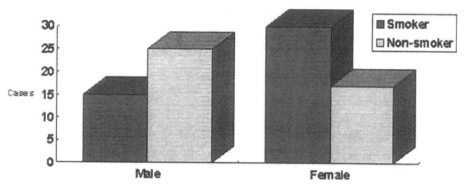

Figure 11.1.   Sample Bar Chart Showing Smoking Habit by Gender.

- Separate cells (bars) by a space.
- Cells may have more than one bar.
- Provide a legend that defines the bars.
- Label the x and y axes.

PIE CHARTS

Pie charts use either quantitative or qualitative data (American Psychological Association 1995, 143). The pie chart represents a single series of data, with each component of the series represented by a wedge proportional to its frequency in the series. Pie charts are used to provide a visual comparison of the frequency of quantitative and/or categorical data in a given series. A variation of a pie chart is the exploded pie chart, where one or more pieces of the pie are raised above the others. A sample pie chart is shown in Figure 11.2.

Some general guidelines to follow when constructing a pie chart are listed below:

- Provide a title for the pie chart.
- Provide a legend for the slices of the pie indicating categories that they represent.

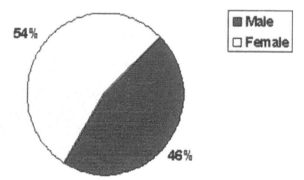

Figure 11.2.   Sample Pie Chart Showing Percentage of Cases by Gender.

- Provide the percentages that the various slices represent.
- Try to avoid using more than 10 component values in the series.
- One pie should represent 100 percent of the series.

Presenting Inferential Statistics

Inferential statistics have their own unique formats for conveying to the audience the importance of the information obtained from the statistical procedure. The minimal information and the manner in which it is displayed is fairly consistent. Previous chapters have examined a variety of inferential procedures. Each will be discussed in terms of how the results obtained from the procedure should be displayed.

Z TESTS AND T TESTS

As you recall, z tests and t tests can be used to test hypotheses concerning means. The comparisons can be between two groups or a mean can be tested against a known or expected value. In either case, when reporting the results, one must include the obtained test score, the means that were being tested, the number of cases the means were based on, and the significance level that was tested. When using t tests, the researcher must also report the degrees of freedom that were used to determine the cutoff score for the t test.

Example Results from a Paired t-Test Procedure

Suppose that a researcher collected data on blood lead levels from a group of workers before and after a new fume hood was installed. The researcher wanted to determine if there was a significant difference between the average blood lead levels for the workers before and after installing the new fume hoods. Results from the paired t test indicated the average blood lead level was 20 mg/dl before and 8 mg/dl after. The obtained t score was 2.40, with degrees of freedom of 23. In the example the researcher would report the results as follows:

$$(t = 2.40, df = 23, P < .05)$$

ONE-WAY ANALYSIS OF VARIANCE

In a one-way analysis of variance (ANOVA) procedure, the researcher wishes to determine if there are significant differences in the average scores when comparing them by groups. The researcher should report the sources of variation, sum of squares, degrees of freedom, mean squares, and F ratio. The following table is the typical format for presenting the results of an ANOVA procedure. The footnote to the table indicates significance of the F ratio.

ANOVA Summary Table

Source of Variation	Sum of Squares	Df	Mean Squares	F Ratio
Between	145.6	2	72.8	22.750*
Within	38.4	12	3.2	
Total	184.0	14		

*P < .05.

CORRELATION PROCEDURES

Correlation procedures are described in terms of their correlation coefficient, which can be represented by a variety of symbols depending on the specific correlation procedure being used. If, for example, Pearson's correlation procedure is being used, the correlation coefficient is represented by an r. If the phi coefficient is being used, the symbol ϕ would be used. When reporting results from correlation procedures, the obtained coefficient and an indication as to whether it is significant must be reported. Typically, the following format is used to report correlation coefficients:

$$(r = .05, P < .05)$$

REGRESSION PROCEDURES

Regression procedures follow the same format as the correlation procedures in reporting the results. In addition to the coefficient and its significance, regression procedures may also include the equation of the line, a scatterplot depicting the cases, and the fitted regression line.

NONPARAMETRIC PROCEDURES

Nonparametric procedures are reported in the same manner as parametric procedures. The obtained test score, the chi-square value for that test score, the degrees of freedom used in the procedure, and an indication as to whether the test results are significant should be reported. For example, if a researcher performed a chi-squared procedure on a set of data, the following would be reported:

$$(\chi^2 = 3.04, df = 2, P > .05)$$

Using Computer Software to Develop Presentations

There are a variety of software programs available to present research data. The Microsoft Office program lends itself well to data analysis and data presentation. While not all of the statistical procedures presented in this book can be calculated using Office, it is an excellent beginning point for the safety researcher.

Microsoft Excel allows the researcher to perform a variety of descriptive statistics as well as many inferential statistics. The data analysis tools for Excel are located under the "Tools" category on the main toolbar. To begin, click on "Tools" and go down to the bottom of the list to "Data Analysis." If "Data Analysis" does not appear, go to "Add Ins" under "Tools" and check the "Data Analysis" boxes. This should add "Data Analysis" as an option under "Tools." Some of the statistical procedures one can perform using Excel include descriptive statistics, ANOVA, t tests, regressions, and correlations, to name a few.

In addition to these statistical procedures, Excel can also be used to generate a variety of charts that can also be imported into Word documents and Power Point presentations.

SAMPLE DATA ANALYSIS USING MICROSOFT EXCEL

To develop a presentation using Microsoft Office, the first step is to arrange the data in an Excel spreadsheet. The following data was obtained from a sample of males and females:

Male	Female
3	4
4	6
3	5
4	4
6	6
5	6
5	5
7	4
4	3
5	3

The first step is to input the data into a spreadsheet as depicted above. Next, to calculate descriptive statistics for the data, click on "Tools," then "Data Analysis." In the list of procedures, you will see "Descriptive Statistics." Click on that, then click "OK." A new box will appear asking you for the input range. Highlight the two columns of the spreadsheet that contain your data, including the column labels. Click on the box that says "Summary Statistics," then click "OK."

The following new sheet will appear:

Male		Female	
Mean	4.6	Mean	4.6
Standard error	0.4	Standard error	0.371184
Median	4.5	Median	4.5
Mode	4	Mode	4

Male		Female	
Standard deviation	1.264911064	Standard deviation	1.173788
Sample variance	1.6	Sample variance	1.377778
Kurtosis	−0.026041667	Kurtosis	−1.45663
Skewness	0.543516473	Skewness	−0.04122
Range	4	Range	3
Minimum	3	Minimum	3
Maximum	7	Maximum	6
Sum	46	Sum	46
Count	10	Count	10

You may have to widen the columns so that all of the information is visible. The summary statistics function calculates all of the descriptive statistics discussed in Chapter 4 of this book.

The next step is to perform a t test on the data. The t test will determine if there is a significant difference between the average for males and the average for females. To perform the t test, click on sheet 1, which contains the raw data table. Next, to calculate descriptive statistics for the data, click on "Tools," then "Data Analysis." In the list of procedures, you will see "T Test: Two Sample Assuming Equal Variances." Click on that, then click "OK." A new box will appear asking you for the input range. Highlight the column containing the data for males. Then click in the box asking for the second set of data and highlight the column containing the information for females. The hypothesized mean difference should be "0" since we are looking for any difference, and a check should be in the "labels" box since we have data labels in the first row. Click on the box that says "Summary Statistics," then click "OK."

The following sheet will appear:

t Test: Two Sample Assuming Equal Variances

	Male	Female
Mean	4.6	4.6
Variance	1.6	1.377777778
Observations	10	10
Pooled variance	1.488888889	
Hypothesized mean difference	0	
Df	18	
t Stat	0	
$P(T \leq t)$ one-tail	0.5	
t Critical one-tail	1.734063062	
$P(T \leq t)$ two-tail	1	
t Critical two-tail	2.100923666	

The obtained t value is equal to 0, and since we are performing a two-tailed test (the average for males is equal to the average for females), we are interested in the line that says "$P(T \leq t)$ two-tail," which is 1.00. This indicates that the probability of obtaining the results we obtained is equal to $1.00 \times 100\%$, or a 100% chance, meaning the results are not significant. We would have to obtain a value less than .05 in order for the results to be considered significant.

DEVELOPING PRESENTATIONS USING MICROSOFT OFFICE

Another feature of Microsoft Office is the ability to incorporate charts and graphs from Excel into papers and presentations. In Excel, the "Chart Wizard" can be used to develop a number of different types of charts and graphs. Using the data in a spreadsheet, a chart can be easily constructed. With the raw data sheet open, click on the "Chart Wizard" tool box located on the main tool bar. The Chart Wizard will take you through the steps of constructing a column chart to depict your data. The chart can then be incorporated into a Word document or PowerPoint presentation by copying and pasting.

Chapter Summary

Tables and charts can be used to provide a graphic representation of the data in a study. While they can be used to help illustrate essential points about descriptive statistics and data when used properly, they have specific formats that should be followed to ensure data are properly displayed.

Tables can be used to summarize data in a study. They should include row and column totals and complete information about the data contained within. Pie charts and column charts are used to graphically display data. Pie charts summarize one variable and are used to summarize data on a total population. Column charts can be used to make comparisons between several categorical variables.

Chapter Review Exercises

1. What are tables used for?
2. What are some basic guidelines to use when developing a table, bar chart, or pie chart?
3. What type of data are used in a bar chart?
4. What type of data are used in a pie chart?

For each of the examples presented below, what is the appropriate type of chart or table that would summarize the data?

5. A researcher collected data from a sample of 300 components and found that 21 were defective.
6. A safety manager surveyed 300 employees and found that in Department A, 95% had no symptoms of carpal tunnel syndrome, while 5% did. In Department B, 92% had no symptoms, compared to 7% who did.

Appendixes: Statistical Tables

Appendix A: Cumulative Distribution Function for the Standard Normal Random Variable

z	.00	.01	.02	.03	.04	.05	.06	.07	.08	.09
-3.4	.0003	.0003	.0003	.0003	.0003	.0003	.0003	.0003	.0003	.0002
-3.3	.0005	.0005	.0005	.0004	.0004	.0004	.0004	.0004	.0004	.0003
-3.2	.0007	.0007	.0006	.0006	.0006	.0006	.0006	.0005	.0005	.0005
-3.1	.0010	.0009	.0009	.0009	.0008	.0008	.0008	.0008	.0007	.0007
-3.0	.0013	.0013	.0013	.0012	.0012	.0011	.0011	.0011	.0010	.0010
-2.9	.0019	.0018	.0018	.0017	.0016	.0016	.0015	.0015	.0014	.0014
-2.8	.0026	.0025	.0024	.0023	.0023	.0022	.0021	.0021	.0020	.0019
-2.7	.0035	.0034	.0033	.0032	.0031	.0030	.0029	.0028	.0027	.0026
-2.6	.0047	.0045	.0044	.0043	.0041	.0040	.0039	.0038	.0037	.0036
-2.5	.0062	.0060	.0059	.0057	.0055	.0054	.0052	.0051	.0049	.0048
-2.4	.0082	.0080	.0078	.0075	.0073	.0071	.0069	.0068	.0066	.0064
-2.3	.0107	.0104	.0102	.0099	.0096	.0094	.0091	.0089	.0087	.0084
-2.2	.0139	.0136	.0132	.0129	.0125	.0122	.0119	.0116	.0113	.0110
-2.1	.0179	.0174	.0170	.0166	.0162	.0158	.0154	.0150	.0146	.0143
-2.0	.0228	.0222	.0217	.0212	.0207	.0202	.0197	.0192	.0188	.0183
-1.9	.0287	.0281	.0274	.0268	.0262	.0256	.0250	.0244	.0239	.0233
-1.8	.0359	.0351	.0344	.0336	.0329	.0322	.0314	.0307	.0301	.0294

z									
−1.7	.0446	.0436	.0427	.0418	.0409	.0401	.0392	.0384	.0375	.0367
−1.6	.0548	.0537	.0526	.0516	.0505	.0495	.0485	.0475	.0465	.0455
−1.5	.0668	.0655	.0643	.0630	.0618	.0606	.0594	.0582	.0571	.0559
−1.4	.0808	.0793	.0778	.0764	.0749	.0735	.0721	.0708	.0694	.0681
−1.3	.0968	.0951	.0934	.0918	.0901	.0885	.0869	.0853	.0838	.0823
−1.2	.1151	.1131	.1112	.1093	.1075	.1056	.1038	.1020	.1003	.0985
−1.1	.1357	.1335	.1314	.1292	.1271	.1251	.1230	.1210	.1190	.1170
−1.0	.1587	.1562	.1539	.1515	.1492	.1469	.1446	.1423	.1401	.1379
−0.9	.1841	.1814	.1788	.1762	.1736	.1711	.1685	.1660	.1635	.1611
−0.8	.2119	.2090	.2061	.2033	.2005	.1977	.1949	.1922	.1894	.1867
−0.7	.2420	.2389	.2358	.2327	.2293	.2266	.2236	.2206	.2177	.2148
−0.6	.2743	.2709	.2676	.2643	.2611	.2578	.2546	.2514	.2483	.2451
−0.5	.3085	.3050	.3015	.2981	.2946	.2912	.2877	.2843	.2810	.2776
−0.4	.3446	.3409	.3372	.3336	.3300	.3264	.3228	.3192	.3156	.3121
−0.3	.3821	.3783	.3745	.3707	.3669	.3632	.3594	.3557	.3520	.3483
−0.2	.4207	.4168	.4129	.4090	.4052	.4013	.3974	.3936	.3897	.3859
−0.1	.4602	.4562	.4522	.4483	.4443	.4404	.4364	.4325	.4286	.4247
−0.0	.5000	.4960	.4920	.4880	.4840	.4801	.4761	.4721	.4681	.4641

Source: Stephen Kpkoska and Christopher Nevison, *Statistical Tables and Formulae* (New York: Springer Verlag, 1989), 55–56.

z	.00	.01	.02	.03	.04	.05	.06	.07	.08	.09
0.0	.5000	.5040	.5080	.5120	.5160	.5199	.5239	.5279	.5319	.5359
0.1	.5398	.5438	.5478	.5517	.5557	.5596	.5636	.5675	.5714	.5753
0.2	.5793	.5832	.5871	.5910	.5948	.5987	.6026	.6064	.6103	.6141
0.3	.6179	.6217	.6255	.6293	.6331	.6368	.6406	.6443	.6480	.6517
0.4	.6554	.6591	.6628	.6664	.6700	.6736	.6772	.6808	.6844	.6879
0.5	.6915	.6950	.6985	.7019	.7054	.7088	.7123	.7157	.7190	.7224
0.6	.7257	.7291	.7324	.7357	.7389	.7422	.7454	.7486	.7517	.7549
0.7	.7580	.7611	.7642	.7673	.7704	.7734	.7764	.7794	.7823	.7852
0.8	.7881	.7910	.7939	.7967	.7995	.8023	.8051	.8078	.8106	.8133
0.9	.8159	.8186	.8212	.8238	.8264	.8289	.8315	.8340	.8365	.8389
1.0	.8413	.8438	.8461	.8485	.8508	.8531	.8554	.8577	.8599	.8621
1.1	.8643	.8665	.8686	.8708	.8729	.8749	.8770	.8790	.8810	.8830
1.2	.8849	.8869	.8888	.8907	.8925	.8944	.8962	.8980	.8997	.9015
1.3	.9032	.9049	.9066	.9082	.9099	.9115	.9131	-9147	.9162	.9177
1.4	.9192	.9207	.9222	.9236	.9251	.9265	.9279	.9292	.9306	.9319
1.5	.9332	.9345	.9357	.9370	.9382	.9394	.9406	.9418	.9429	.9441
1.6	.9452	.9463	.9474	.9484	.9495	.9505	.9515	.9525	.9535	.9545
1.7	.9554	.9564	.9573	.9582	.9591	.9599	.9608	.9616	.9625	.9633

z										
1.8	.9641	.9649	.9656	.9664						
1.9	.9713	.9719	.9726	.9732						
2.0	.9772	.9778	.9783	.9788						
2.1	.9821	.9826	.9830	.9834						
2.2	.9861	.9864	.9868	.9871						
2.3	.9893	.9896	.9898	.9901						
2.4	.9918	.9920	.9922	.9925						
2.5	.9938	.9940	.9941	.9943						
2.6	.9953	.9955	.9956	.9957						
2.7	.9965	.9966	.9967	.9968						
2.8	.9974	.9975	.9976	.9977						
2.9	.9981	.9982	.9982	.9983						
3.0	.9987	.9987	.9987	.9988						
3.1	.9990	.9991	.9991	.9991						
3.2	.9993	.9993	.9994	.9994	.9994	.9994	.9994	.9995	.9995	.9995
3.3	.9995	.9995	.9995	.9996	.9996	.9996	.9996	.9996	.9996	.9997
3.4	.9997	.9997	.9997	.9997	.9997	.9997	.9997	.9997	.9997	.9998

Source: Stephen Kokoska and Christopher Nevison, *Statistical Tables and Formulae* (New York: Springer Verlag, 1989), 55–56.

Appendix B: Critical Values for the t Distribution

ν	.20	.10	.05	.025	.01	.005	.001	.005	.001	.0001
1	1.3764	3.0777	6.3138	12.7062	31.8205	63.6567	318.3088	636.6192	3183.0988	
2	1.0607	1.8856	2.9200	4.3027	6.9646	9.9248	22.3271	31.5991	70.7001	
3	.9785	1.6377	2.3534	3.1824	4.5407	5.8409	10.2145	12.9240	22.2037	
4	.9410	1.5332	2.1318	2.7764	3.7469	4.6041	7.1732	8.6103	13.0337	
5	.9195	1.4759	2.0150	2.5706	3.3649	4.0321	5.8934	6.8688	9.6776	
6	.9057	1.4398	1.9432	2.4469	3.1427	3.7074	5.2076	5.9588	8.0248	
7	.8960	1.4149	1.8946	2.3646	2.9980	3.4995	4.7853	5.4079	7.0634	
8	.8889	1.3968	1.8595	2.3060	2.8965	3.3554	4.5008	5.0413	6.4420	
9	.8834	1.3830	1.8331	2.2622	2.8214	3.2498	4.2968	4.7809	6.0101	
10	.8791	1.3722	1.8125	2.2281	2.7638	3.1693	4.1437	4.5869	5.6938	
11	.8755	1.3634	1.7959	2.2010	2.7181	3.1058	4.0247	4.4370	5.4528	
12	.8726	1.3562	1.7823	2.1788	2.6810	3.0545	3.9296	4.3178	5.2633	
13	.8702	1.3502	1.7709	2.1604	2.6503	3.0123	3.8520	4.2208	5.1106	
14	.8681	1.3450	1.7613	2.1448	2.6245	2.9768	3.7874	4.1405	4.9850	
15	.8662	1.3406	1.7531	2.1314	2.6025	2.9467	3.7328	4.0728	4.8800	
16	.8647	1.3368	1.7459	2.1199	2.5835	2.9208	3.6862	4.0150	4.7909	
17	.8633	1.3334	1.7396	2.1098	2.5669	2.8982	3.6458	3.9650	4.7144	
18	.8620	1.3304	1.7341	2.1009	2.5524	2.8784	3.6105	3.9216	4.6480	

19	.8610	1.3277	1.7291	2.0930	2.5395	2.8609	3.5794	3.8834	4.5899
20	.8600	1.3253	1.7247	2.0860	2.5280	2.8453	3.5518	3.8495	4.5385
21	.8591	1.3232	1.7207	2.0796	2.5176	2.8314	3.5271	3.8192	4.4929
22	.8583	1.3212	1.7171	2.0739	2.5083	2.8187	3.5050	3.7921	4.4520
23	.8575	1.3195	1.7139	2.0687	2.4999	2.8073	3.4850	3.7676	4.4152
24	.8569	1.3178	1.7109	2.0639	2.4922	2.7969	3.4668	3.7454	4.3819
25	.8562	1.3163	1.7081	2.0595	2.4851	2.7874	3.4502	3.7251	4.3517
26	.8557	1.3150	1.7056	2.0555	2.4786	2.7787	3.4350	3.7066	4.3240
27	.8551	1.3137	1.7033	2.0518	2.4727	2.7707	3.4210	3.6896	4.2987
28	.8546	1.3125	1.7011	2.0484	2.4671	2.7633	3.4081	3.6739	4.2754
29	.8542	1.3114	1.6991	2.0452	2.4620	2.7564	3.3962	3.6594	4.2539
30	.8538	1.3104	1.6973	2.0423	2.4573	2.7500	3.3852	3.6460	4.2340
40	.8507	1.3031	1.6839	2.0211	2.4233	2.7045	3.3069	3.5510	4.0942
50	.8489	1.2987	1.6759	2.0086	2.4033	2.6778	3.2614	3.4960	4.0140
60	.8477	1.2958	1.6706	2.0003	2.3901	2.6603	3.2317	3.4602	3.9621
120	.8446	1.2886	1.6577	1.9799	2.3578	2.6174	3.1595	3.3735	3.8372
ω	.8416	1.2816	1.6449	1.9600	2.3263	2.5758	3.0902	3.2905	3.7190

Source: Stephen Kpkoska and Christopher Nevison, *Statistical Tables and Formulae* (New York: Springer Verlag, 1989), 57.

Appendix C: Critical Values for the Chi-square Distribution

Chi-square Table

v	.10	.05	.025	.01	.005	.001	.0005	.0001
1	2.7055	3.8415	5.0239	6.6349	7.8794	10.8276	12.1157	15.1367
2	4.6052	5.9915	7.3778	9.2103	10.5966	13.8155	15.2018	18.4207
3	6.2514	7.8147	9.3484	11.3449	12.8382	16.2662	17.7300	21.1075
4	7.7794	9.4877	11.1433	13.2767	14.8603	18.4668	19.9974	23.5121
5	9.2364	11.0705	12.8325	15.0863	16.7496	20.5150	22.1053	25.7448
6	10.6446	12.5916	14.4494	16.8119	18.5476	22.4577	24.1028	27.8563
7	12.0170	14.0671	16.0128	18.4753	20.2777	24.3219	26.0178	29.8775
8	13.3616	15.5073	17.5345	20.0902	21.9550	26.1245	27.8680	31.8276
9	14.6837	16.9190	19.0228	21.6660	23.5894	27.8772	29.6658	33.7199
10	15.9872	18.3070	20.4832	23.2093	25.1882	29.5883	31.4198	35.5640
11	17.2750	19.6751	21.9200	24.7250	26.7568	31.2641	33.1366	37.3670
12	18.5493	21.0261	23.3367	26.2170	28.2995	32.9095	34.8213	39.1344
13	19.8119	22.3620	24.7356	27.6882	29.8195	34.5282	36.4778	40.8707
14	21.0641	23.6848	26.1189	29.1412	31.3193	36.1233	38.1094	42.5793
15	22.3071	24.9958	27.4884	30.5779	32.8013	37.6973	39.7188	44.2632
16	23.5418	26.2962	28.8454	31.9999	34.2672	39.2524	41.3081	45.9249
17	24.7690	27.5871	30.1910	33.4087	35.7185	40.7902	42.8792	47.5664
18	25.9894	28.8693	31.5264	34.8053	37.1565	42.3124	44.4338	49.1894
19	27.2036	30.1435	32.8523	36.1909	38.5823	43.8202	45.9731	50.7955
20	28.4120	31.4104	34.1696	37.5662	39.9968	45.3147	47.4985	52.3860
21	29.6151	32.6706	35.4789	38.9322	41.4011	46.7970	49.0108	53.9620
22	30.8133	33.9244	36.7807	40.2894	42.7957	48.2679	50.5111	55.5246
23	32.0069	35.1725	38.0756	41.6384	44.1813	49.7282	52.0002	57.0746

24	33.1962	36.4150	39.3641	42.9798	45.5585	51.1786	53.4788	58.6130
25	34.3816	37.6525	40.6465	44.3141	46.9279	52.6197	54.9475	60.1403
26	35.5632	38.8851	41.9232	45.6417	48.2899	54.0520	56.4069	61.6573
27	36.7412	40.1133	43.1945	46.9629	49.6449	55.4760	57.8576	63.1645
28	37.9159	41.3371	44.4608	48.2782	50.9934	56.8923	59.3000	64.6624
29	39.0875	42.5570	45.7223	49.5879	52.3350	58.3012	60.7346	66.1517
30	40.2560	43.7730	46.9792	50.8922	53.6720	59.7031	62.1619	67.6326
31	41.4217	44.9853	48.2319	52.1914	55.0027	61.0983	63.5820	69.1057
32	42.5847	46.1943	49.4804	53.4858	56.3281	62.4872	64.9955	70.5712
33	43.7452	47.3999	50.7251	54.7755	57.6484	63.8701	66.4025	72.0296
34	44.9032	48.6024	51.9660	56.0609	58.9639	65.2472	67.8035	73.4812
35	46.0588	49.8018	53.2033	57.3421	60.2748	66.6188	69.1986	74.9262
36	47.2122	50.9985	54.4373	58.6192	61.5812	67.9852	70.5881	76.3650
37	48.3634	52.1923	55.6680	59.8925	62.8833	69.3465	71.9722	77.7977
38	49.5126	53.3835	56.8955	61.1621	64.1814	70.7029	73.3512	79.2247
39	50.6598	54.5722	58.1201	62.4281	65.4756	72.0547	74.7253	80.6462
40	51.8051	55.7585	59.3417	63.6907	66.7660	73.4020	76.0946	82.0623
50	63.1671	67.5048	71.4202	76.1539	79.4900	86.6608	89.5605	95.9687
60	74.3970	79.0819	83.2977	88.3794	91.9517	99.6072	102.6948	109.5029
70	85.5270	90.5312	95.0232	100.4252	104.2149	112.3169	115.5776	122.7547
80	96.5782	101.8795	106.6286	112.3288	116.3211	124.8392	128.2613	135.7825
90	107.5650	113.1453	118.1359	124.1163	128.2989	137.2084	140.7823	148.6273
100	118.4980	124.3421	129.5612	135.8067	140.1695	149.4493	153.1670	161.3187

Source: Stephen Kokoska and Christopher Nevison, *Statistical Tables and Formulae* (New York: Springer Verlag, 1989), 59.

Appendix D: Critical Values for the *F* Distribution

v_2	v_1 = 1	2	3	4	5	6	7	8	9	10	15	20	30	40	60	120	ω
1	161.45	199.50	215.71	224.58	230.16	233.99	236.77	238.88	240.54	241.98	245.95	248.01	250.10	251.14	252.20	253.25	254.25
2	18.51	19.00	19.16	19.25	19.30	19.33	19.35	19.37	19.38	19.40	19.43	19.45	19.46	19.47	19.48	19.49	19.50
3	10.13	9.55	9.28	9.12	9.01	8.94	8.89	8.85	9.81	8.79	8.70	8.66	8.62	8.59	8.57	8.55	8.53
4	7.71	6.94	6.59	6.39	6.26	6.16	6.09	6.04	6.00	5.93	5.86	5.80	5.75	5.72	5.69	5.66	5.63
5	6.61	5.79	5.41	5.19	5.05	4.95	4.88	4.82	4.77	4.74	4.62	4.43	4.50	4.46	4.43	4.40	4.37
6	5.99	5.14	4.76	4.53	4.39	4.28	4.21	4.15	4.10	4.06	3.94	3.87	3.81	3.77	3.74	3.70	3.67
7	5.59	4.74	4.35	4.12	3.97	3.87	3.79	3.73	3.68	3.64	3.51	3.44	3.38	3.34	3.30	3.27	3.23
8	5.32	4.46	4.07	3.64	3.60	3.58	3.50	3.44	3.39	3.35	3.22	3.15	3.08	3.04	3.01	2.97	2.93
9	5.12	4.26	3.86	3.63	3.48	3.37	3.29	3.23	3.18	3.14	3.01	2.94	2.86	2.83	2.79	2.75	2.71
10	4.96	4.10	3.71	3.48	3.35	3.22	3.14	3.07	3.02	2.98	2.85	2.77	2.70	2.66	2.62	2.58	2.54
11	4.84	3.98	3.59	3.36	3.20	3.09	3.01	2.95	2.90	2.85	2.72	2.65	2.57	2.53	2.49	2.45	2.41
12	4.75	3.89	3.49	3.26	3.11	3.00	2.91	2.85	2.80	2.75	2.62	2.54	2.47	2.43	2.38	2.34	2.30
13	4.67	3.81	3.41	3.18	3.03	2.92	2.83	2.77	2.71	2.67	2.b3	2.46	2.38	2.34	2.30	2.25	2.21
14	4.60	3.74	3.34	3.11	2.96	2.85	2.76	2.70	2.65	2.60	2.46	2.39	2.31	2.27	2.22	2.18	2.13
15	4.54	3.68	3.29	3.06	2.90	2.79	2.71	2.64	2.59	2.54	2.40	2.33	2.25	2.20	2.16	2.11	2.07
16	4.49	3.63	3.24	3.01	2.85	2.74	2.66	2.59	2.54	2.49	2.35	2.28	2.19	2.15	2.11	2.06	2.01
17	4.45	3.59	3.20	2.96	2.81	2.70	2.61	2.55	2.49	2.41	2.31	2.23	2.15	2.10	2.06	2.01	1.96
18	4.41	3.55	3.16	2.93	2.77	2.66	2.58	2.51	2.46	2.41	2.27	2.19	2.11	2.06	2.02	1.97	1.92
19	4.38	3.52	3.13	2.90	2.74	2.63	2.54	2.48	2.42	2.38	2.23	2.16	2.07	2.03	1.98	1.93	1.88
20	4.35	3.49	3.10	2.87	2.71	2.60	2.51	2.45	2.39	2.35	2.20	2.12	2.04	1.99	1.95	1.90	1.85
21	4.32	3.47	3.07	2.84	2.6	2.57	2.49	2.42	2.37	2.32	2.18	2.10	2.01	1.96	1.92	1.87	1.82
22	4.30	3.44	3.05	2.82	2.66	2.55	2.46	2.40	2.34	2.30	2.15	2.07	1.98	1.94	1.89	1.94	1.79
23	4.28	3.42	3.03	2.80	2.64	2.53	2.44	2.37	2.32	2.27	2.13	2.05	1.96	1.91	1.86	1.81	1.76
24	4.26	3.40	3.01	2.78	2.62	2.51	2.42	2.36	2.30	2.25	2.11	2.03	1.94	1.89	1.84	1.79	1.74
25	4.24	3.39	2.99	2.76	2.60	2.49	2.40	2.34	2.28	2.24	2.09	2.01	1.92	1.87	1.82	1.77	1.71
30	4.17	3.32	2.92	2.69	2.53	2.42	2.33	2.27	2.21	2.16	2.01	1.93	1.84	1.79	1.74	1.68	1.63
40	4.08	3.23	2.84	2.61	2.45	2.14	2.25	2.18	2.12	2.08	1.92	1.84	1.74	1.69	1.64	1.58	1.51
50	4.03	3.18	2.79	2.56	2.40	2.34	2.20	2.13	2.07	2.03	1.87	1.78	1.69	1.63	1.58	1.51	1.44
60	4.00	3.15	2.76	2.53	2.17	2.25	2.17	2.10	2.04	1.99	1.84	1.75	1.65	1.59	1.53	1.47	1.39
120	3.92	3.07	2.68	2.45	2.29	2.18	2.09	2.02	1.96	1.91	1.75	1.66	1.55	1.50	1.43	1.35	1.26
ω	3.85	3.00	2.61	2.38	2.22	2.10	2.11	1.94	1.88	1.84	1.67	1.58	1.46	1.40	1.32	1.23	1.00

Source: Stephen Kpkoska and Christopher Nevison, *Statistical Tables and Formulae* (New York: Springer Verlag, 1989), 60.

Appendix E: Table of Random Units

	(1)	(2)	(3)	(4)	(5)	(6)	(7)	(8)	(9)	(10)	(11)	(12)	(13)	(14)
1	10480	15011	01536	02011	81647	91646	69179	14194	62590	36207	20969	99570	91291	90700
2	22368	46573	25595	85393	30995	89198	27982	53402	93965	34091	52666	19174	39615	99505
3	24130	48360	22527	97265	76393	64809	15179	24830	49340	32081	30680	19655	63348	58629
4	42167	93093	06243	61680	07856	16376	39440	53537	71341	57004	00849	74917	97758	16379
5	37570	39975	81837	16656	06121	91782	60468	81305	49684	60672	14110	06927	01263	54613
6	77921	06907	11008	42751	27756	53498	18602	70659	90655	15053	21916	81825	44394	42880
7	99562	72905	56420	69994	98872	31016	71194	18738	44013	48840	63213	21069	10634	12952
8	96301	91977	05463	07972	18876	20922	94595	56869	69014	60045	18425	84903	42508	32307
9	89579	14342	63661	10281	17453	18103	57740	84378	25331	12566	58678	44947	05585	56941
10	85475	36857	43342	53988	53060	59533	38867	62300	08158	17983	16439	11458	18593	64952
11	28918	69578	88231	33276	70997	79936	56865	05859	90106	31595	01547	85590	91610	78188
12	63553	40961	48235	03427	49626	69445	18663	12695	52180	20847	12234	90511	33703	90322
13	00429	93969	52636	92737	88974	33488	36320	17617	30015	08272	84115	27156	30611	74952
14	10365	61129	87529	85689	48237	52267	67689	93394	01511	26358	85104	20285	29975	89868
15	07119	97336	71048	08178	77233	13916	47564	81056	97735	85977	29372	74461	28551	90707
16	51085	12765	51821	51259	77452	16308	60756	92144	49442	53900	70960	63990	75601	40719
17	02368	21382	52404	60268	89368	19885	55322	44819	01188	65255	64835	44919	05944	55157
18	01011	54092	33362	94904	31273	04146	18594	29852	71585	85030	51132	01915	92747	64951
19	52162	53916	46369	58586	23216	14513	83149	98736	23495	64350	94738	17752	35156	35749
20	07056	97628	33787	09998	42698	06691	76988	13602	51851	46104	88916	19509	25625	68104
21	48663	91245	85828	14346	09172	30168	90229	04734	59193	22178	30421	61666	99904	32812
22	54164	58492	22421	74103	47070	25306	76468	26384	58151	06646	21524	15227	96909	44592
23	32639	32363	05597	24200	13363	38005	94342	28728	35806	06912	17012	64161	18296	22851
24	29334	27001	87637	87308	58731	00256	45834	15398	46557	41135	10367	07684	36188	18510
25	02488	33062	28834	07351	19731	92420	60952	61280	50001	67658	32586	86679	50720	94953

(continued)

Appendix E (continued)

	(1)	(2)	(3)	(4)	(5)	(6)	(7)	(8)	(9)	(10)	(11)	(12)	(13)	(14)
26	81525	72295	04839	96423	24878	82661	66566	14778	76791	14780	13300	87074	79666	96725
27	29676	20591	68086	26432	46901	20849	89768	81536	86645	12659	92259	57102	80428	25280
28	00742	57392	39064	66432	84673	40027	32832	61362	98947	96067	64760	64584	96096	98253
29	05366	04213	25669	26422	44407	44048	37937	63904	45766	66134	75470	66520	34693	90449
30	91921	26418	64117	94305	26766	25940	39972	22209	71500	64568	91402	42416	07844	69618
31	00582	04711	87917	77341	42206	35126	74081	99547	81817	42607	43808	76655	62028	76630
32	00725	69884	62797	56170	86324	88072	76222	36086	84637	93161	76038	65855	77919	88006
33	69011	65797	95876	55293	18988	27354	26575	08625	40801	59920	21841	80150	12777	48501
34	25976	57948	29888	88644	67917	48708	18912	82271	65424	69774	33611	54262	85963	03547
35	09763	83473	73577	12908	30883	18317	28290	35797	05998	41688	34952	17888	38917	88050
36	91567	42595	27958	30134	04024	86385	29880	99730	55536	84855	29080	09250	79656	73211
37	17955	56349	90999	49127	20044	59931	06115	20542	18059	02008	73708	83517	36103	42791
38	46503	18584	19845	49618	02304	51038	20655	58727	28168	54715	56942	53389	20562	87338
39	92157	89634	94824	78171	84610	82834	09922	25417	44137	48413	25555	21246	15509	20468
40	14577	62765	356405	81263	39667	47358	56873	56307	61607	49518	89656	20103	77490	18062
41	98427	07523	33362	64270	01638	92417	66969	98420	04880	45585	46565	04102	46890	45709
42	34914	63976	88720	82765	34476	17032	87589	40836	32427	70002	70663	88863	77775	69348
43	70060	28277	39475	46473	23219	53416	94970	25832	69915	94884	19661	72828	00102	66794
44	53976	54914	06990	67245	68350	82948	11398	42878	80287	88267	47363	46634	06541	97809
45	76072	29515	40980	07391	58745	25774	22987	80059	39911	96189	41151	14222	60697	59583
46	90725	52210	83974	29992	65831	38837	50490	83765	55657	14361	31720	57375	56228	41546
47	64364	67412	33339	31926	14883	24413	59744	92351	97473	89286	35931	04110	23728	51900
48	08962	00358	31662	25388	61642	34072	81249	35648	56891	69352	48373	45578	78547	81788
49	95102	68379	93526	70765	10593	04542	76463	54328	02349	17247	28865	14777	62730	92277
50	15664	10493	20492	38391	91132	21999	59516	81652	27195	48223	46751	22923	32261	85653

Source: William Beyer, ed. *Standard Mathematical Tables and Formulae.* 29th ed. (Boca Raton. FL: CRC Press), 523.

Glossary of Terms

Alpha Levels: The alpha (α) level is the probability of committing a Type I error. When using inferential statistics, the researcher tries to control the probability of making these errors.

Alternative Hypothesis: The alternative hypothesis postulates that there are significant differences in the population or sample being examined. The null hypothesis is represented by the term "H_0," while the alternative hypothesis is represented by the term "H_i." For each null hypothesis, there is a corresponding alternative hypothesis.

Bar Charts: Bar charts are a method of displaying nominal or ordinal data, such as age, sex, etc.

Bias: A bias is anything in the selection process that results in a group of people who for whatever reason are not considered to be representative of the population.

Binomial Distribution: In situations where there are only two possible outcomes for an event, such as a "heads/tails" or "yes/no" situation, the distribution is considered to be binomial.

Blind Studies: Blind studies are studies where the participants do not know if they are receiving the treatment. They are used to control participant biases.

Categorical Data: Categorical data are variables that can be described by using categories. Within the categorical data, there are also data referred to as dichotomous, meaning two categories. Categorical data are also referred to as discrete data.

Chi-square Distribution: The chi-square distribution is a distribution used to make inferences about a single population variance. The chi-square is always a squared quantity, so the values will always be positive. The chi-square distribution also utilizes degrees of freedom, which are determined by the statistical test.

Chi-square Test for Goodness of Fit: The chi-square test for goodness of fit determines if obtained proportions in a sample are significantly different from what could be expected due to chance.

Chi-square Test of Independence: The chi-square test of independence can be used with data in which each subject is measured on two categorical variables. The test assumes a chi-square distribution. The statistical procedure follows the same type of process as does the chi-square goodness of fit, in which the observed frequency of cases in each cell is compared to an expected number.

Chunk Sampling: In chunk sampling, the researcher selects people who happen to be present in a particular location at a particular time.

Cluster Sample: A cluster sample is a selection of subjects from representative geographic areas.

Cochran's Q Test: Cochran's Q test is used to determine rankings over a series of items for a given population.

Coefficient of Determination: The coefficient of determination (r^2) is derived by squaring the correlation coefficient. This gives the researcher an indication of the amount of variability in the dependent variable that can be directly attributed to the independent variable.

Compound Probabilities: Compound probabilities are probabilities used in situations where one must determine the probability of the occurrence of different events, but, instead of determining the failure due to all events occurring at the same time, a person wishes to determine the occurrence of any one of a number of events at a time.

Conditional Probabilities: In a conditional probability, some condition or restriction is placed on the sample that is being used to determine the probability.

Control Group: The group in the experiment that does not receive any type of treatment.

Correlation Procedure: A correlation procedure indicates the degree of association between two or more variables. The association means that there is some relationship between the variables. It does not show cause and effect.

Data: Recorded observations gathered for the purposes of a statistical study.

Deductive Research: Research where a model is developed and then tested using data collected from observations.

Dependent Variable: A dependent variable is a variable that can be influenced or changed by other variables under study.

Descriptive Statistics: Descriptive statistics consists of the techniques that are used to summarize and describe quantitative measurements taken for a population or sample.

Double Blind Studies: Studies where neither the participant nor the researcher, or the person administering the treatments, knows who is receiving the treatment. They are used to control biases from the participants and those taking measurements.

Eta Coefficient: The eta coefficient provides an estimate of the degree of association between a nominal variable grouped by an interval variable.

Experiment: An experiment is a process carried out under controlled conditions to test research hypotheses. Experiments using control groups are used when one wishes to show cause and effect relationships.

Experimental Group: The group in an experiment that receives the treatment being tested.

F Distribution: The F distribution compares two population variances in the form of a ratio called an F ratio. The F ratio is actually formed by the ratio of two chi-square variables, each divided by its own degree of freedom.

Frequencies: Frequencies are the numbers of times an event occurs.

Frequency Polygons: A frequency polygon is a depiction of the histogram column points. The frequency polygon can be developed using the results from the histogram.

Histograms: A histogram is a column chart depicting the data from the frequency distribution.

Independent Variable: An independent variable is a variable that measures characteristics that cannot be influenced or changed.

Inductive Research: Inductive research is when we make our observations and then create the model to fit what we have observed.

Inferential Statistics: Inferential statistics uses the results from a subset or sample to infer the results to a larger group or population.

Interquartile Range: The interquartile range is a measure of variability. This range is the middle 50% of all observations in the distribution. It is the distance between the end of the first quartile and the beginning of the fourth quartile.

Interval Data: Interval data is considered a form of continuous data. Interval data has zero as a placeholder on the scale. An example of an interval scale is the scale on a Fahrenheit thermometer.

Joint Event: A joint event is an event in which the researcher asks what the probability of event A and event B occurring at the same time is. To determine this, the researcher must multiply the probability of the independent events together.

Likert-type Scale: Likert-type scales are used to measure ordinal variables. They typically present five or six degrees of possible agreement, with the endpoints being opposites.

Mean: The mean is the arithmetic average of a distribution of numbers.

Median: The median is the point at which 50% of the values lie above and 50% of the values lie below.

Mode: The mode of a distribution is the most frequently occurring number in the distribution.

Nonparametric Statistics: Nonparametric statistics is statistics used when the data cannot be assumed to follow a particular distribution. These tests are also referred to as distribution-free tests. Nonparametric statistics is typically used with ordinal and categorical data.

Normal Distribution: A normal distribution is a distribution that can be represented by a bell-shaped curve. Characteristics such as intelligence, the histogram of the data, and subsequent frequency polygon can be considered to follow a normal distribution.

Null Hypothesis: The null hypothesis states that there is no statistically significant difference in the population or samples under examination.

One-way Analysis of Variance: A one-way analysis of variance (ANOVA) procedure is used to test hypotheses that compare more than two means. The ANOVA procedure uses an *F* ratio statistic to determine if there are significant differences between the means being tested. To determine where the significance lies between the means, follow-up or post hoc tests must be performed.

Ordinal Data: Ordinal data is rank-order data. Ordinal means "order"; ordinal data allow the researcher to order the data in some fashion.

Placebo: A placebo is a substance that is intended to have no effect on the subject in an experiment. It has no real value in its application. It is used to ensure that the treatment is the actual cause for the differences between the control and experimental groups and not a psychological effect of being treated or being a part of the study.

Paired *t* Test: The paired *t* test can be used to test hypotheses involving two means, just like the *z* test. The major difference between the two tests is with the number of cases involved. *t* tests are used when the number of cases does not meet a minimum of 25. The hypotheses can also test whether a sample mean is significantly greater, less than, or different from a given population mean.

Pearson Correlation Coefficient: The Pearson correlation coefficient is one of a number of bivariate correlation procedures. It is used when one wishes to correlate two variables, both of which are continuous in nature.

Pie Charts: Pie charts are charts where each single series of data is represented by a wedge proportional to its frequency in the series. Pie charts use either quantitative or qualitative data.

Phi Coefficient: The phi coefficient is used to rank two dichotomous variables. A dichotomous variable is one that has only two possible outcomes, such as yes/no, male/female, etc.

Point Biserial Correlation: The point biserial correlation coefficient provides an estimate of the degree of association between an interval grouped by a dichotomous variable.

Poisson Probability: Poisson probabilities are used to determine the probability of an event when the frequency of its occurrence is quite low compared to the overall exposure. The Poisson probability function is probably one of the most important for the safety professional.

Population: A population is the all-inclusive group of subjects that have the characteristics a researcher is interested in observing.

Probability: Probability is the chance that an event will occur.

Prospective Studies: Prospective studies examine the future outcomes of events. The data are collected and analyzed, and conclusions about how the results should turn out in the future are formulated.

Qualitative Measures: Qualitative measures provide an indication of the qualities or characteristics of a subject. Examples of qualitative measures include the gender of a person or the color of a sign.

Quantitative Measures: Measures that describe a characteristic in terms of a number. Quantitative measures include the age of a person measured in years and the number of accidents an organization had over the previous year.

Rating Scales: Questions using rating scales present respondents with words or phrases and ask them to indicate the extent to which the words or phrases describe their feelings. There are several variations on rating scales.

Random Samples: A random sample is a sample where each person who is selected from the population has an equal chance of being selected.

Ratio Data: Ratio data is continuous data. In this scale, zero is not a placeholder, but represents absence of the characteristic.

Range: The range of a data set is the difference between the lowest-value and the highest-value data points.

Regression: Regression procedures allow a person to develop prediction equation that can be used to predict dependent variables from independent variables. With regression, a correlation coefficient is first derived and then an equation for the line that best fits the data points can be calculated.

Retrospective Studies: A retrospective study examines past events to determine the factors that influenced them.

Sample: In statistics, a sample is a subset of the total population. The sample is representative of the population in terms of the variable under investigation. The properties of the sample are studied in order to gain an understanding of the entire population.

Scheffe's S Test: Scheffe's S test is one of the more conservative post hoc tests. Scheffe's S test tests not only pairwise comparisons but also all the a posteriori contrasts among means. To determine if a pair of means are significantly different from one another, the absolute difference between the pair of means are compared to a critical value.

Semantic Differential: The semantic differential is a seven-step rating scale anchored by opposite objectives.

Simple Event: In simple probability, the researcher compares the number of times an event occurred to the total number of possible outcomes.

Simple Random Samples: Simple random samples are samples that have been selected following a process of enumerating all subjects in the population, then selecting those whose number has been selected to be included in the sample.

Spearman Rank-Order Correlation Coefficient: The Spearman rank-order correlation coefficient is used to determine correlations between ranked or ordinal data.

Standard Deviation: The standard deviation is considered the average difference from the mean for the scores in a distribution.

Statistical Power: Statistical power is the probability of being able to correctly determine if a null hypothesis is false. Otherwise stated, it is how accurately a statistical test can identify significance when it truly exists.

Statistics: The branch of mathematics that deals with the collection, tabulation, and systematic classification of data.

Stratified Random Sample: A stratified random sample is a sample that is selected from a population that was first broken down into groups or strata. Subjects are then randomly selected from each group, ensuring a representative sampling by group.

Subject: Individual or single observation in a study; also referred to as a case.

Survey Research: Survey research is a systematic method for obtaining information from a population. Forms of data collection in survey research include written survey forms, personal interviews, and telephone interviews.

Table: A table is a set of data that is arranged in rows and columns. The purpose of a table is to present the frequency at which some event occurs in different categories or subdivisions of a variable.

***t* Distribution:** The *t* distribution has been developed to perform hypothesis testing with a small numbers of cases. For the purposes of this text and as has been defined by other statisticians, a small number of cases can be considered to be that fewer than 25.

***t* Test:** The *t* test can be used to test hypotheses involving two means, just like the *z* test. The major difference between the two tests is with the number of cases involved. *t* tests are used when the number of cases does not meet a minimum of 25.

Two-tailed Test: When a researcher tests for significant differences between groups, then the test is considered a two-tailed test. Significance levels for two-tailed tests use both the upper and lower ends of the curve. If the result of the statistical test lands in the shaded regions of the curve, then it is considered to be significant.

Type I Error: A Type I error occurs when the statistical test incorrectly indicates to the researcher that the null hypothesis is false and as a result, the researcher rejects the null hypothesis and accepts the alternative.

Type II Error: A Type II error occurs when the researcher incorrectly accepts the null hypothesis when the null hypothesis is false.

Variance: The variance of a distribution is a measure of how much the individual data points vary from the distribution mean. The variance is the average of the squared deviations from the mean.

Volunteer Sample: In a volunteer sample, the participants volunteer their participation in the study. An example of a volunteer sample is a local television station that asks people to call in with their vote.

Wilcoxon Rank-Sum Test: The Wilcoxon rank-sum test tests whether there are significant differences between sets of ranks. The rankings are compared between two sets of independent populations, and if there is a significant Wilcoxon rank-sum test result, one can conclude that there are significant differences in the sum of the ranks when comparing the two groups.

z Scores: A z score can be used to identify the location of a raw score on the normal distribution curve. The z scores can then be used with a z table to determine percentages of populations and probabilities associated with the normal distribution.

z Tests: The z test can be used to test hypotheses involving two means. The hypotheses can test whether a sample mean is significantly greater, less than, or different from a given population mean.

References

American Psychological Association. 1994. *Publication Manual of the American Psychological Association: Fourth Edition*. Washington, DC: American Psychological Association.

Backstrom, Charles and Gerald Hursh-Cesar. 1981. *Survey Research*. New York: Macmillan.

Cohen, Jacob, and Patricia Cohen. 1983. *Applied Multiple Regression/Correlation Analysis for the Social Sciences*. Hillsdale, NJ: Erlbaum.

Freedman, David, Robert Pisani, and Roger Purves. 1978. *Statistics*. New York: Norton.

Hays, William. 1988. *Statistics*. Orlando: Holt, Rinehart and Winston.

Horvath, Theodore. 1974. *Basic Statistics for the Behavioral Sciences*. Glenview, IL: Scott, Foresman.

Kirk, Roger. 1982. *Experimental Design*. Belmont, CA: Wadsworth.

Kuzma, Jan. 1992. *Basic Statistics for the Health Sciences*. Mountain View, CA: Mayfield.

Witte, Robert and John Witte. 1997. *Statistics*. Fort Worth: Harcourt Brace College.

Solutions to Selected Sample Problems

Chapter 1

1. Describe the differences between a retrospective study, a prospective study, and an experiment.

> A retrospective study examines past events to determine the factors that influenced those events. Prospective studies examine the outcomes of events that will occur in the future. An experiment is another format for a research study. An experiment using a control group is a method used when one wishes to show cause-and-effect relations. The main features of an experiment are the presence of a control group, an experimental group, and random selection of subjects.

2. Describe the differences between an independent variable and a dependent variable.

> A dependent variable is a variable that can be influenced or changed by other variables under study. An independent variable is a variable that measures characteristics that cannot be influenced or changed.

3. Describe the situations in which a researcher would use a simple random sample versus a cluster sample and a stratified random sample.

> Random selection is one of the best ways of ensuring that there are no biases in the method used to select subjects for participation in the study.
> A cluster sample is used when the researcher wishes to select a representative sample from geographic areas.
> In a stratified random sample, the researcher anticipates that there may be differences in the results based on the subjects' memberships in particular groups.

4. In each of the following cases, identify the dependent variable and the independent variable:

    grade on exam (dependent)   hours studied (independent)
    training programs conducted   accident frequency (dependent)
        (independent)

5. Define the following terms:

    Bias: Bias is anything in the selection process that results in a group of people who are not considered to be representative of the population.
    Placebo: A placebo is a treatment that has no effects on the subjects. A placebo is used to ensure that the treatment is the actual cause for the differences between the control and experimental groups and not a result of being treated or part of the study.
    Variable: A variable is any measurement that can have a potential range of values.
    Population: A population is the all-inclusive group of subjects that have the characteristics the researcher is interested in observing.
    Statistic(s): (1) A statistic is a numerical term that summarizes or describes a sample. (2) Statistics is defined as the science that deals with the collection, tabulation, and systematic classification of data.
    Double blind study: A study where neither the person conducting the study nor the subject knows if the subject is really receiving a treatment.

6. A researcher wishes to show that a particular drug really works. What must the researcher do to show cause and effect?

    The researcher must conduct an experiment using a control and an experimental group.

7. A researcher wishes to conduct a survey to identify people's perceptions of the economy in the United States. What type of sampling technique would be most appropriate and why?

    A cluster sample would be most appropriate because one may assume that there are geographic differences in people's perceptions about the economy.

8. The researcher wishes to perform a simple random sample selection using 100 people from a population of 1,000. Describe the process the researcher should go through to complete this task.

    Number the subjects from 1 to 1,000. Using a random numbers table, go down the first column reading the first 4 digits of the random number. Those subjects whose assigned number appears are selected until 100 people have been chosen.

9. Not shown.

10. For each of the following examples, provide the best format for a research study:

   A researcher wishes to identify past accident trends for an organization.
   A researcher wishes to determine if back belts really work.
   Researchers wish to set up a study wherein they measure performance in such a manner that their potential biases do not affect the outcomes.

   Double blind study

11. When a researcher makes an observation and then creates a model to match it, the type of research is

   b. inductive research

12. A researcher designed a study with a treatment group and a control group. This type of research is

   a. an experiment

13. A researcher enumerated the sample, then used a table to select the cases. The type of sample selected is a

   b. simple random sample

14. The sampling method that accounts for geographic differences in the population is a

   a. cluster sample

15. An example of a nonprobability sample is a

   c. chunk sample

16. Not shown.

17. A researcher wishes to randomly select five subjects from a population of 1,000 using a simple random selection. Using the random numbers table in Appendix A, identify the first five subjects that would be in the sample. Describe the process used to perform this selection.

   Starting in the first column and continuing down each of the columns until five subjects are selected, the first five would be:

   429, 365, 961, 997, 922

18. Compare and contrast chunk sampling to stratified random sampling.

Chunk sampling is a nonprobability sampling technique in which the researcher selects from a group. Stratified random sampling is considered a probability technique in which subjects are first arranged according to a group, then randomly selected from each.

19. Not shown.

20. Not shown.

21. Describe the differences between a population and a sample.

A population is the all-inclusive group with a particular trait or characteristic. A sample is a subset of the population.

Chapter 2

1. A safety manager decided to perform a quality check on a product that was being produced by the company. He randomly selected 15 units from a box of 100 and found 3 to be damaged. What is the probability of a damaged piece of equipment coming off the production line?

$$3/15 = .20, \text{ or } 20\%$$

2. A system was set up in parallel with two components, A and B. The probability of failure for A is .20 and for B is .10. In order for the system to fail, both must fail. What is the probability of a system failure?

$$P_A \text{ and } P_B = .20 \times .10 = .02, \text{ or } 2\%$$

3. A system was set up in series with two components, A and B. In order for the system to fail, only one must fail. The probability of failure for A is .30 and for B is .20. What is the probability of a system failure?

$$P_A \text{ or } P_B = .30 + .20 - (.30 \times .20) = .44 \text{ or } 44\%$$

4. A system was found to average a rate of 2 failures per 30,000 hours of use. What is the probability of one failure to the system in the next 40,000 hours?

$$P_x = \frac{2.718^{-2.67} \, 2.67^1}{1} = .18, \text{ or } 18\% \text{ chance}$$

$$M = (40,000)(2/30,000) = 2.67$$

5. A system is arranged in parallel with four components. If two components have a probability of failure of .007 and the other two have a probability of failure of .003, what is the probability of a system failure if all components have to fail at the same time?

$$P \text{ (Failure)} = .007 \times .007 \times .003 \times .003 = 4.41 \times 10^{-10}$$

6. There are seven subjects in a study. Three have a disease and four are disease-free. What is the probability of selecting a person with the disease?

$$3/7 = .43, \text{ or } 43\%$$

7. What is the probability of selecting a club from a deck of cards?

$$13/52 = .25, \text{ or } 25\%$$

8. You have eight poker chips, six red and two blue. What is the probability of selecting one red chip?

$$P \text{ (Selecting a red chip)} = 6/8 = .75 \text{ or } 75\%$$

9. A researcher measures a person's IQ. The IQ can be considered:

   b. a variable

10. $(1/6) \times (1/6) =$

    d. 1/36

Chapter 3

1. Describe the process one would follow to set up a frequency distribution.

   Arrange the values from lowest to highest. Establish equal ranges for the data values. Count the number of cases for each data range, then set up a table with the ranges and the frequency of cases in each range.

2. What information would a frequency distribution provide a researcher?

   An indication of the distribution of scores in a sample.

3. What information would a frequency polygon provide?

   Graphical depiction of the distribution of scores in a distribution.

4. Using the following data set, develop a frequency distribution.

34, 33, 35, 36, 56, 54, 54, 55, 56, 34, 56

Range	Frequency
0–20	0
21–40	5
41–60	6
Total	20

5. Give an example of a data set in which a normal distribution would be assumed.

   IQ scores on a test with a large number of cases

6. Give an example of a data set in which a *t* distribution would be assumed.

   Test scores from a small sample (fewer than 25 cases)

7. Give an example of a data set in which a binomial distribution would be assumed.

   Determining the probability of heads or tails when flipping a coin.

8. Develop a histogram for the following data.

   9, 4, 2, 5, 7, 5, 10, 12, 12, 3, 3, 2, 6, 4, 2

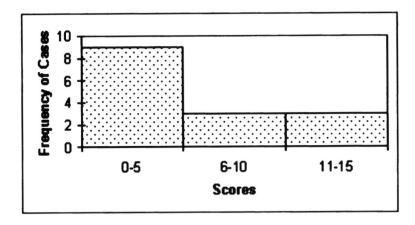

9. A safety manager collected data for a process and found that in a batch of items, there was a 20% chance that a component was defective. The safety manager wishes to know, if he selects 6 components at a time, what the probability of selecting 0, 1, 2, 3, 4, 5, and 6 failed components is in a selection of 6 components.

Probability Results

$$P(0 \text{ Failures}) = \frac{6!}{0! \, (6 - 0)!} \, (.20^0)(1 - .20)^{6 - 0} = .26$$

$$P(1 \text{ Failures}) = \frac{6!}{1!(6 - 1)!} \, (.20^1)(1 - .20)^{6 - 1} = .39$$

$$P(2 \text{ Failures}) = \frac{6!}{2!(6 - 2)!} \, (.20^2)(1 - .20)^{6 - 2} = .24$$

$$P(3 \text{ Failures}) = \frac{6!}{3!(6 - 3)!} \, (.20^3)(1 - .20)^{6 - 3} = .08$$

$$P(4 \text{ Failures}) = \frac{6!}{4!(6 - 4)!} \, (.20^4)(1 - .20)^{6 - 4} = .02$$

$$P(5 \text{ Failures}) = \frac{6!}{5!(6 - 5)!} \, (.20^5)(1 - .20)^{6 - 5} = .002$$

$$P(6 \text{ Failures}) = \frac{6!}{6!(6 - 6)!} \, (.20^6)(1 - .20)^{6 - 6} = .00006$$

10. Develop the cumulative frequency distribution for the scenario presented in Exercise 9.

Value	Probability	Cumulative Probability
0	.26	.260
1	.39	.650
2	.24	.890
3	.08	.980
4	.02	1.000
5	.002	1.000
6	.00006	1.000
Total		1.000

Chapter 4

Use the following data set to complete the exercises 1–3: (3, 5, 8, 10, 4, 6, 3, 16, 19, 12).

1. What is the mean?

8.6

2. What is the standard deviation?

    5.58

3. What percentage of the population is expected to score above 9?

$$Z = (9 - 8.6)/5.58 = .07, (47\%)$$

4. What is the mean of the following distribution?

$$(3, 6, 8, 12, 14, 19, 17, 3, 6, 2)$$

    9.00

5. What percentage of the population is expected to score below 5?

$$Z = (5 - 9)/6.13 = -.65, (26\%)$$

6. Within which two scores is 95% of the population expected to score?

$$-1.96 = \overline{X} - 9/6.13 = -3$$
$$1.96 = \overline{X} - 9/6.13 = 21$$

7. What is the 99% confidence interval for this data?

$$C.I. (99\%) = 9 +/- (2.58)(6.13/\sqrt{10}) = (4, 14)$$

8. What percentage of the population is expected to obtain a z score of at least 1.56?

    .94 (94%)

9. How many possible combinations can you obtain with seven items (a different order signifies a different combination)?

$$7! = 5,040$$

10. Fred has 10 cars, each of a different color. If he decided to select 3 at a time, how many combinations could he come up with? (Order is not important.)

$$\frac{10!}{(3!)(10-3)!} = 120$$

11. How many combinations can he have with different orders?

$$\frac{10!}{(10-3)!} = 720$$

12. Calculate the variance of the following data set.

$$2, 13, 17, 15, 19, 23, 4, 6, 7, 8$$

$$\sigma^2 = 49.1$$

13. Calculate the standard deviation of this data set.

$$\sigma = 7.0$$

14. What is the range of this data set?

$$23 - 2 = 21$$

15. A manufacturer of computer chips checks for faulty chips as they come off the production line. In a typical workshift, for every 10,000 chips produced, there are 4 damaged chips identified. A salesperson sold the company a new piece of equipment that he claimed would produce a better-quality chip with fewer defects. After allowing the machine to operate for 3 days, 125,000 chips were produced and 43 defects were identified. Does the new machine produce significantly fewer defective chips than the old one?

$$P_{(x)} = \frac{2.718^{-50} \ 50^{43}}{43!} = .04, \text{ or } 4\%$$

$M = (125,000)(4/10,000) = 50$
Yes, the machine produces significantly fewer defects.

Chapter 5

1. Develop null and alternative hypotheses for the following situation: A safety manager wishes to know if there are significantly more accidents in department A than in department B.

   H_0: The average for A is less than or equal to the average for B.
   H_1: The average for A is greater than the average for B.

2. Develop null and alternative hypotheses for the following situation: An ergonomist wishes to determine if there is a significant difference between the average number of repetitive-motion injuries for Plant A and Plant B.

$$H_0: \overline{X}_A = \overline{X}_B$$
$$H_1: \overline{X}_A \neq \overline{X}_B$$

3. Develop null and alternative hypotheses for the following situation: A safety trainer wishes to know if the average test scores for Group A are significantly lower than those for Group B.

H_0: The average for A is greater or equal to the average for B.
H_1: The average for A is less than the average for B.

4. Describe the differences between a Type I error and a Type II error.

In a Type I error, the researcher rejects the null hypothesis when it is actually true. In a Type II Error, the researcher fails to reject the null hypothesis when it is false.

5. What is the α level used for?

It determines the probability of correctly rejecting the null hypothesis when the null hypothesis is false.

6. Describe the seven steps required to perform a statistical test.

Develop a statistical hypothesis.
Choose the appropriate statistical test or procedure.
Determine the Statistical Distribution.
Determine significance levels.
Formulate a decision rule.
Run the statistical test.
Formulate a conclusion and make a decision.

7. What does β represent?

It is the probability of committing a Type II error.

8. What is the difference between a one-tailed test and a two-tailed test?

A one-tailed test tests greater-than or less-than hypotheses. Two-tailed tests test for significant differences in either direction.

9. Give an example of a hypothesis that would be tested as a one-tailed test.

H_0: The average of A is less than or equal to the average of B.
H_1: The average of A is greater than the average of B.

10. Not shown.
11. Give an example of a hypothesis that would be tested as a two-tailed test.

H_0: The average of A is equal to the average of B.
H_1: The average of A is not equal to the average of B.

12. What critical value on the normal distribution would give the researcher 99% above the point and 1% below?

   ±2.33

13. What critical value on the normal distribution would give the researcher 95% below the point and 5% above?

   ±1.96

Chapter 6

1. Describe the situations in which a researcher would choose the z test over a t test.

   z tests are used for large samples ($N > 25$) that can assume a normal distribution, while t tests are used for small samples where these assumptions cannot be met.

2. Provide an example of a null and alternative hypothesis for each of the following procedures.

   Where $N > 25$
   H_0: The average of A is less than or equal to the average of B.
   H_1: The average of A is greater than the average of B.

   t test
   Where $N < 25$
   H_0: The average of A is less than or equal to the average of B.
   H_1: The average of A is greater than the average of B.

   One-way ANOVA

   H_0: Mean of Group 1 = Mean of Group 2 = Mean of Group 3
   H_1: Mean of Group 1 ≠ Mean of Group 2 ≠ Mean of Group 3

3. What critical score should a researcher use if he is running a z test for the following null and alternative hypotheses (assuming α level = .05)?

   Null Hypothesis: The mean difference scores are equal to zero (no difference).
   Alternative Hypothesis: The mean difference scores are not equal to zero (significantly different).
   Assuming α level = .05, the critical score would be ±1.96.

4. What critical score should a researcher use if he is running a *t* test for the following null and alternative hypotheses (assuming α level = .05 and df = 30)?

> Null Hypothesis: The difference scores are greater than or equal to zero.
> Alternative Hypothesis: The difference scores are less than zero.
> Assuming α level = .05 and df = 30, the critical score would be 1.70.

5. What information is used to determine the critical score for a one-way ANOVA?

> The $df_{between}$ and the df_{within} are used to identify the critical score on the *F* table.

6. A trainer wishes to compare the average test score for his class to the national averages. The trainer believes his class scored significantly higher than the average. The national average is 86% (SD = 10, N = 100), and his class scored 94% with a standard deviation of 3.0. Assume an α level of .05 and a sample size of 50. Provide the hypothesis being tested, the rejection rule, the results, and the decision that one should make on the basis of the results.

> 1. Hypotheses
> H_0: The average for the class is less than or equal to the national average.
> H_1: The average for the class is greater than the national average.
> 2. Select Test.
>   Use the *z* test because there is a large number of cases (n > 25).
> 3. Select the normal distribution.
> 4. Assuming an α level of .05 and a one-tailed test, the critical score is 1.65.
> 5. The trainer will reject the null hypothesis and accept the alternative if the obtained *z* test is greater than 1.65.
> 6. Calculate *z*.

$$z = \frac{94 - 86}{\sqrt{\dfrac{9}{50} + \dfrac{100}{100}}} = 7.36$$

> 7. Conclusion
>   Reject the null hypothesis and accept the alternative because the obtained *z* test value is greater than the cutoff score. The trainer can conclude the class average is significantly higher than the national average.

7. A training manager collected data from a group of 10 subjects. Each subject was observed and the number of unsafe acts was recorded. The subjects then partici-

pated in a safety awareness training program. They were again observed, and the unsafe acts recorded. How would the manager set up a statistical test to determine if there were any changes in the unsafe acts observed?

The training manager can use a t test to determine if there is a significant difference in the before and after scores using a paired t test procedure.

8. A safety manager wanted to determine if there was a significant difference in the average number of accidents before lunch than after. He compared the average number of accidents of two groups of employees. The manager recorded the number of accidents for 20 employees before lunch and 20 different employees after lunch. Each month, one group averaged 2 accidents with a standard deviation of 0.03 before lunch while the other group averaged 3 accidents with a standard deviation of 0.15 after lunch. Are there significantly more accidents for the after-lunch group? Provide the hypothesis being tested, the rejection rule, the results, and the decision that one should make on the basis of the results. Use an α level of .05.

1. Hypotheses
   H_0: The average number of errors is less than or equal to the number before.
   H_1: The average number of errors is greater after lunch than before.
2. Select test.
   Use the t test since there is a small number of cases ($n < 25$).
3. Select the t distribution.
4. Assuming an α level of .05 and a one-tailed test, the df = 38, and the critical score is 1.69.
5. The researcher will reject the null hypothesis and accept the alternative if the obtained t test is greater than 1.69.
6. Calculate t.

$$Sp = \frac{.03^2 (20 - 1) + .15^2 (20-1)}{20 + 20 - 2} = .11$$

$$t = \frac{3 - 2}{.11 \sqrt{\frac{1}{20} + \frac{1}{20}}} = 28.7$$

7. Conclusion
   Reject the null hypothesis and accept the alternative because the obtained t test value is greater than the cutoff score. The safety manager can conclude that the average number of accidents reported by the group after lunch is significantly greater than the average number of accidents reported by the group before lunch.

9. An environmental researcher believed that there were significantly different blood lead levels for children living in three different buildings in a housing complex. The researcher ran an ANOVA procedure and obtained the following results:

Source of Variation	df	Sum of Squares	Mean Squares	F
Between	2	14,230	7,115	1.74
Within	9	36,720	4,080	
Total	11	50,950		

Provide the seven steps for the analysis. What conclusions should be drawn from this study?

1. Hypotheses
   H_0: The average levels in all homes are equal.
   H_i: The average levels in all homes are not equal.
2. Select test.
   Choose the ANOVA test because the researcher is testing the means for three different locations.
3. Select the F distribution for the ANOVA.
4. Assuming an α level of .05 and that the degrees of freedom are 2 and 11, the critical score is 3.59.
5. The researcher will reject the null hypothesis and accept the alternative if the obtained F ratio is greater than 3.59.
6. Carry out a one-way ANOVA.
   An F ratio of 1.74 was obtained.
7. Conclusion
   Do not reject the null hypothesis because the obtained F ratio is not greater than the critical score. There is no significant difference in the average blood levels for the three locations.

10. What t score would give a researcher 10% of the population at each end of the curve and 80% of the cases in the middle section? (Assume df = 24.)

$$t = 1.318$$

11. A researcher was performing a one-way ANOVA. He identified the df_{within} to be 15 and the $df_{between}$ to be 4. What is the critical score, assuming the α level = .05?

$$F = 3.06$$

Chapter 7

1. What are the data requirements for using the Pearson correlation procedure?

   Two variables, both measured on the interval or ratio scale, normally distributed.

2. What are the data requirements for using the point biserial correlation procedure?

> Two variables, one measured on a dichotomous categorical level, the other measured on a continuous scale.

3. Not shown.
4. What is regression used for?

> Regression is used to predict a dependent variable from an independent variable.

5. How would one interpret a correlation coefficient of .80 compared to −.80?

> Both are equally strong correlations. The positive correlation indicates that as the values for the independent variable increase, the values for the dependent variable also increase. For the −.80 correlation, as the values for the independent variable increase, the values for the dependent variable decrease.

6. An investigator obtained a correlation coefficient of .60. What must be done to determine if this is significant?

> A follow-up t test must be performed on the correlation coefficient.

7. Describe the relation between correlation coefficients, significance tests, and the coefficient of determination and why all three are important when making decisions concerning correlation coefficients.

> A strong correlation coefficient can account for a great proportion of variability in the dependent variable through the independent variable. However, it may not be significant. On the other hand, a correlation coefficient may be significant but be considered too weak and to account for very little variability in the dependent variable through the independent variable.

8. Subjects were asked to complete a Cumulative Trauma Disorder (CTD) scale (high score represents many CTD symptoms, low score represents few CTD symptoms) and to disclose how many times they missed work each month. The following descriptive statistics were obtained:

Variance of x = 155
Variance of y = .40
Mean of x = 65
Mean of y = 2.7
r = .62

If there were 200 subjects in this study, would the correlation coefficient be significant?

1. Hypotheses.
   Null Hypothesis: The correlation coefficient equals 0.
   Alternative Hypothesis: The correlation coefficient is not equal to 0.
2. Select test.
   Choose the t test for correlations.
3. Select the t distribution.
4. Assuming an α level of .05 and degrees of freedom of 198, the critical score is 1.97.
5. The researcher will reject the null hypothesis and accept the alternative if the obtained t score is greater than 1.97.
6. Calculate t.

$$t = \frac{.62}{.11\sqrt{\dfrac{1}{20} + \dfrac{1}{20}}} = 11.12$$

7. Conclusion
   Reject the null hypothesis because the obtained t score is greater than the critical score. The correlation coefficient is significant.

9. A regression equation was calculated on safety training scores and the number of safety infractions in 1 year. The equation derived was as follows:

$$y = .09x + 1.02$$

What is the expected number of safety infractions of someone with a safety training score of 27?

$$y = .09x + 1.02$$

$$y = .09(27) + 1.02 = 3.45 \text{ safety infractions}$$

10. A safety manager wished to determine whether there was a relation between the department employees belonged to and their subjective rating for wrist pain using a 10-point scale: 1 (little or no pain) to 10 (severe pain). The following data was collected:

Case	Department A	Department B
1	2	7
2	4	6
3	5	8
4	3	9
5	2	10
6	5	7
7	4	5
8	6	6

Case	Department A	Department B
9	3	6
10	2	4
11	4	7
12	1	4
13	3	3
14	5	7
15	3	8
Average	3.47	6.47
Population Standard Deviation	2.23	

11. Is there a relation between department membership and subjective pain levels?

$$r_{pb} = \frac{(3.47 - 6.47)\sqrt{(.50)(.50)}}{2.23} = -.67$$

The results indicate a moderate negative relation between the two departments.

Chapter 8

1. Define nonparametric statistics.

Nonparametric statistics is statistics used when the data cannot be assumed to follow a particular distribution.

2. Describe the data requirements for nonparametric statistics.

Nonparametric statistics is typically used with ordinal and categorical data. It is also referred to as distribution-free tests.

3. Describe the process one would follow when using the χ^2 test of independence.

The observed frequencies in each cell are compared to the frequencies that were expected. If there are significant differences between the obtained versus expected results, then the test would be significant.

4. Describe the process one would follow when using the Wilcoxon rank-sum test.

The Wilcoxon rank-sum test tests whether there are significant differences between sets of ranks.

5. Describe the process one would follow when using the χ^2 goodness of fit test.

χ^2 tests are used with categorical data and assume a χ^2 distribution.
χ^2 test for goodness of fit tests to see if obtained proportions in a sample are significantly different from what could be expected due to chance.

6. What are the data requirements for the χ^2 goodness of fit test?

The data must be measured on the frequency level and grouped.

7. What statistical test is used to test for a significant Wilcoxon rank-sum?

The z test is used to determine if the Wilcoxon rank-sum is significant.

8. What hypothesis is tested to determine significance in a Wilcoxon rank-sum test?

Null Hypothesis: The sum of the ranks for the two groups is equal.
Alternative Hypothesis: The sum of the ranks for the two groups is not equal.

9. How would one adjust for ties in the Wilcoxon rank-sum test?

For tied rankings, the ranks that the numbers will occupy are added up and then divided by the number of ties.

10. What is the critical score for a χ^2 test with 15 degrees of freedom and an α level of .05?

$$\chi^2 = 25.00$$

11. How would one calculate the degrees of freedom for a χ^2 test that uses a 4 × 3 table?

$$df = (4 - 1)(3 - 1) = 6$$

12. A safety manager collected data from 50 employees who used back belts as a regular part of their job. She asked them if they felt the back belt fit properly, which they responded to as yes or no. She then broke the sample down into three departments. The data collected were as follows:

Back Belt Fit Properly	Department A	Department B	Department C
Yes	12	8	14
No	8	11	16

What conclusions can be drawn?

1. Hypotheses
   Null Hypothesis: Observed frequency of cases in the cells equals the expected frequency of cases in the cells.
   Alternative Hypothesis: Observed frequency of cases in the cells does not equal the expected frequency of cases in the cells.
2. Select test.
   Choose the χ^2 test of association
3. Select the χ^2 distribution.
4. Assuming an χ level of .05 and degrees of freedom of 2, the critical score is 5.99.
5. The researcher will reject the null hypothesis and accept the alternative if the obtained χ^2 is greater than 5.99.
6. Calculate χ^2.

$$\chi^2 = \frac{(12-9.9)^2}{9.9} + \frac{(8-9.4)^2}{9.4} + \frac{(14-14.8)^2}{14.8} + \frac{(8-10.1)^2}{10.1} + \frac{(11-9.6)^2}{9.6} + \frac{(16-15.2)^2}{15.2} = 1.37$$

7. Conclusion

Do not reject the null hypothesis since the obtained χ^2 score is not greater than the critical score.

13. A company had five different types of safety glasses for employees to choose from. Assuming there is an equal chance for an employee to choose any of the five types, what conclusions can the safety manager reach on the basis of 50 employees' selection of glasses as shown in the table below?

Glassess	Selected
Type 1	13
Type 2	8
Type 3	7
Type 4	15
Type 5	7

1. Hypotheses
   Null Hypothesis: Observed frequency of cases in the cells equals the expected frequency of cases in the cells.
   Alternative Hypothesis: Observed frequency of cases in the cells does not equal the expected frequency of cases in the cells.

2. Select test.

   Choose the χ^2 goodness of fit test.

3. Select the χ^2 distribution.

4. Assuming an χ level of .05 and the degrees of freedom are 4, the critical score is 9.49.

5. The researcher will reject the null hypothesis and accept the alternative if the obtained χ^2 is greater than 9.49.

6. Calculate χ^2.

$$\chi^2 = \frac{(13 - 10)^2}{10} + \frac{(8 - 10)^2}{10} + \frac{(7 - 10)^2}{10} + \frac{(15 - 10)^2}{10} + \frac{(7 - 10)^2}{10}$$
$$= 5.10$$

7. Conclusion

Do not reject the null hypothesis because the obtained χ^2 score is not greater than the critical score.

Chapter 9

A safety manager put together a survey instrument for a training program. For the following survey items, describe the potential problems and formatting errors that should be addressed before they are used in an instrument.

1. What is your age? _____ 15–20   _____ 20–25   _____ 25–30

   Overlapping categories

2. Did you complete the training program or must you still enroll? _____ yes _____ no

   Asks two questions in one item.

3. What is your overall impression of the program? _____ Good   _____ Bad

   Not all possible answers are available. Better asked as a Likert-type scale item.

4. On a scale of 1 to 5, how would you rate the content? 1 2 3 4 5

   No definition for the rating scale.

5. Using the scale below, please rate your overall satisfaction with the training program.

1	2	3	4	5
Disagree Strongly	Disagree Moderately	Neutral	Agree Moderately	Agree Strongly

The scale does not match the item.

6. Using the scale below, please rate your agreement with the following statement:

This training program was useful.

1	2	3	4	5
Disagree Strongly	Disagree Moderately	Neutral	Agree Moderately	Agree Strongly

Scale is not balanced.

7. Using the scale below, please rate your agreement with the following statement: I will recommend this course to others.

Bad   Good

     1   2   3   4   5   6   7

The scale does not match the item.

8. Describe three major points to provide in a cover letter or at the top of the survey instrument.

The purpose of the survey should be described in a cover letter to the potential respondents or at the top of the survey instrument. This should include the organization that is conducting the survey and the purpose of the study. Overall instructions to the respondents should be provided, such as the time frame they have to respond to the survey, how they return the instrument, etc.

9. What are some benefits of using structured items?

Structured items provide the respondent with a set of possible answers. They generally take less time to answer and code.

10. What does pilot testing do for survey research?

Pilot testing identifies potential problems with a survey instrument and the research design before the study is fully implemented.

Chapter 10

1. What does the term *experimental design* mean?

    The term *experimental design* refers to the plan that is used for assigning experimental conditions to subjects and the statistical analysis associated with the plan.

2. Why is experimental design of importance to someone using literature concerning statistical research?

    By following a set of experimental design guidelines, the researcher can statistically design an experiment that can test several hypotheses and control for various effects that can influence an experiment.

For each of the following experimental designs, summarize the process in conducting a study.

3. One-way ANOVA

    The one-way ANOVA procedure uses one independent variable and one dependent variable. The independent variable is the grouping variable to which subjects are randomly assigned or belong. The dependent variable is the continuous variable and is measured once for each subject in the sample.

4. Completely randomized block design

    In a completely randomized block design, subjects are randomly assigned to the various treatments in an experiment.

5. Randomized block design

    In a randomized block design, the subjects in the experiment are grouped according to a particular characteristic.

6. Latin square design

    To perform a Latin square design, the researcher groups subjects within each level of length of time and groups them according to age within each age category. One restriction for a Latin square design is that the number of groups for the first variable must equal the number of groups for the second blocking variable.

For each of the following studies, what is the experimental design used?

7. A safety manager wanted to determine if there were significant differences in the average number of accidents reported each month for three different plants. Assuming that employment in any one of the three plants is random, what type of design should the manager use?

> ANOVA

8. A safety manager wished to see if safety training could be used to reduce the average number of accidents in one plant. He randomly selected 30 employees and randomly assigned them to one of three different training programs. He then examined the average number of accidents reported for employees by training program attended.

> Completely randomized design

9. The safety manager suspected that the length of employment with the company has an effect on accident involvement. To control for differences in tenure with the company, the manager first divided the employees into one of three groups for length of employment. Then he randomly assigned them to one of three training programs so that each training program had 10 subjects for each of the three length-of-employment categories. He then wanted to determine if the average numbers of accidents reported each month were significantly different from one another.

> Latin square design

Chapter 11

1. What are tables used for?

> Tables are used to present the frequency at which some event occurs in different categories or subdivisions of a variable.

2. What are some basic guidelines to use when developing a table, bar chart, or pie chart?

> One should first examine the format of the data that is going to be displayed. The charts and graphs should be kept simple, they should have titles, and the data displayed in them should be adequately identified.

3. What type of data are used in a bar chart?

> Bar charts provide a visual comparison of quantitative and categorical data. Two or more series of data with multiple categories can be presented on the same chart for comparison purposes.

4. What type of data are used in a pie chart?

> Pie charts use either quantitative or qualitative data. The pie chart repre-
> sents a single series of data, with each component of the series represented
> by a wedge proportional to its frequency in the series.

For each of the examples presented below, what is the appropriate type of chart or
table that would summarize the data?

5. A researcher collected data from a sample of 300 components and found that 21
were defective.

> Pie chart

6. A safety manager surveyed 300 employees and found that in Department A, 95%
had no symptoms of carpal tunnel syndrome, while 5% did. In Department B,
92% had no symptoms, compared to 7% that did.

> Bar chart

Index

95%: confidence interval, 49, 50; critical
    region, 48
99%: confidence interval, 49, 51;
    critical region, 48, 49

alpha level, 55
alternative hypothesis, 53, 54, 59, 60
analysis of variance (ANOVA), 69–79, 87,
    124; decision rule, 73, 78; procedure
    assumptions, 70; procedure formula,
    70–73, 76–78; procedure hypotheses, 70,
    71, 73, 76, 77; table, 70, 71, 73, 77, 79,
    87
averages, formula, 41

bar charts, 130, 131
bell-shaped curve, 31, 35, 38, 42, 58, 70
bias, 6, 7, 49, 109, 112
bimodal curve, 31, 32
binomial: distribution, 32–35; distribution
    example, 32; probabilities, 22–34;
    probability formula, 22
bivariate correlation, 81, 82, 118

case, 3; control studies, 109
categorical data, 39, 40, 97, 130, 131
Chi-square, 36, 37, 97–102; distribution,
    37, 38; test for goodness of fit, 97–100;
    test for goodness of fit assumptions, 98;
    test for goodness of fit formula, 98; test
    for goodness of fit hypothesis, 98; test of
    association, 100; test of association
    assumptions, 100; test of association

formula, 101; test of association
    hypothesis, 100
chunk samples, 10
cluster sample, 8
Cochran's Q test, 105–7; assumptions, 105;
    formula, 106; hypothesis, 105
coefficient of determination, 82
cohort studies, 109
combinations, 21–22, 25; formula, 21
completely randomized: design, 125, 126;
    factorial design, 128
compound event probabilities, 17, 18, 24;
    formula, 18
conditional probabilities, 18, 24; formula, 19
confidence interval, 49–51
continuous data, 40, 67, 68, 70
control group, 5, 109
controls, 5
correlation, 81–93, 119, 135;
    coefficient/significance testing, 89, 90, 92
cover letters, 119
critical region, 46–50, 54, 56, 60, 63, 67
cross section studies, 109
cumulative percentages, 30, 31

data: collection, 110, 112, 116; formats, 39,
    83, 40
decision rule, 57, 58
deductive research, 4
dependent variable, 11, 81–83, 87, 89, 90,
    93, 124–26
descriptive statistics, 2, 39–52, 129, 131,
    134–36

dichotomous data, 39, 83, 85, 87, 114
discrete data, 22, 39
displaying data, 129, 130
distribution, 27–38, 42, 56
double blind studies, 5
drop out bias, 6

equation of a line, 91–92
Eta coefficient, 83, 86, 87; assumptions, 86;
    formula, 86, 87
experiment, 5, 55, 81, 123, 126
experimental: design, 123, 125, 126; group,
    5, 6, 109

F distribution, 37, 38, 73, 75, 78
F ratio, 37, 69, 70, 73, 74, 77, 78, 87, 124,
    125, 132
frequencies, 21, 27, 51, 54, 86, 97, 99–101
frequency: distribution, 27–29, 38; polygon,
    29–31

histograms, 28–31, 35, 70

independent variable, 11, 81–83, 87, 89, 90,
    93, 124, 126
inductive research, 4
inferential statistic, 1, 2, 4, 47, 54–57, 59,
    132, 134
instrument: reliability, 111, 118, 119;
    validity, 111, 118, 119
interquartile range, 44, 45
interval data, 40, 115

joint event: formula, 16; probability, 16, 22

Latin square design, 125, 126
Likert scale, 40, 116

mean, 41, 51, 91
measures: central tendency, 41; variability, 42
median, 41, 42, 44, 51
memory bias, 6
Microsoft: Excel, 134; Office, 133, 134, 136
mode, 41, 42, 51

negative correlation, 81, 82, 85, 88
negatively skewed curve, 32, 33
nonparametric statistics, 97–107
nonprobability sample, 10

normal distribution, 31, 32, 35, 38, 42,
    44–46, 50, 51, 56, 59, 61, 83, 90, 103,
    105
null hypothesis, 53–58

observer bias, 6
one-tailed test, 48, 54, 57, 60, 61, 63, 64, 67
one-way analysis of variance (ANOVA), 69,
    70, 73–75, 77–79, 87, 123, 124, 126,
    132–34; assumptions, 70; formulas,
    70–73
ordered combinations, 20, 21, 25; formula,
    19–21, 24
ordinal data, 39, 40, 84

paired comparisons, 115
participant bias, 6
Pearson correlation coefficient, 82–84,
    89–92; assumptions, 83; formula, 84, 92
percentages, 30, 31, 45–47, 51, 60, 132
percentiles, 30, 31
permission to use human subjects, 121
permutations, 19, 24
Phi coefficient, 85, 86, 133; assumptions,
    86; formula, 86
pie charts, 131
pilot testing, 110, 120, 121
placebo, 5
planning a survey, 109–13
point biserial correlation, 83, 87, 88;
    assumptions, 87; formula, 88
Poisson probability, 23; formula, 23
population, 2, 3, 5
positive correlation, 81, 82
positively skewed curve, 31, 33
post hoc tests, 69, 74
probability, 6, 15
prospective studies, 5

qualitative data, 3, 131
quantitative data, 3
questionnaires, 116, 117

random: numbers table, 7, 8, 9; samples, 7
randomized block design, 125, 126
range, 42
rating scales, 115, 116
ratio data, 40, 115
regression, 90–93, 133

research hypotheses, 2, 123
retrospective studies, 4, 11

sample, 2–8, 10, 11; bias, 6; selection, 6, 7, 10, 11; sizes, 97, 120
sampling techniques, 7, 10
scatterplot, 81, 82
Scheffe's test, 74; decision rule, 75; formula, 75
semantic differential scales, 116
significance level, 64, 132
simple event: formula, 16; probability, 16, 20
simple random samples, 7
slope of a line, 90
Spearman rank-order correlation coefficient, 84–85; assumptions, 85; formula, 85
standard deviation, 17, 42, 44–46, 50, 51, 59, 62–66, 68, 69, 88, 91
statistic, defined, 2
statistical: distributions, 56; notation, 2, 3; populations, 5; power, 55; terms, 3; test, 53–57
stratified random sample, 7, 10
structured survey items, 114
subject, 3, 7
survey: instruments, 110, 111, 113, 116–19; items, 110, 113, 119, 121; research, 9, 109–21; research limitations, 120; research procedures, 117–19

t distribution, 35, 36, 38, 56; degrees of freedom, 35

t table, 63, 67, 90, 92
t test, 62–68; assumptions, 63, 65, 89
t test independent groups, 64; formula, 64, 65; hypotheses, 64
t test, paired, 66; formula, 67, 68; hypotheses, 67
t test, single mean, 63–64; formula, 64; hypotheses, 64
tables, 130, 132–35
treatments, 123, 125,
two-tailed test, 53, 57, 60, 63–65, 67, 68, 90, 103, 105, 135
Type I error, 55, 58, 61, 65, 68
Type II error, 55, 120

unstructured survey items, 114

variance, 3, 37, 42–44, 62, 66
volunteer samples, 10

Wilcoxen rank-sum test, 102–5; assumptions, 102, 103; formula, 103; hypothesis, 103

y intercept, 90, 91

z score formula, 45, 46
z scores, 45–48, 57, 60–62, 103
z table, 45, 46, 60
z test, 59–62, 78, 103, 118; assumptions, 59, 62; formula, 61, 62; hypotheses, 59, 60, 62

About the Author

Christopher A. Janicak is a professor of safety and graduate program coordinator at Indiana University of Pennsylvania. He holds a doctor of philosophy degree in research methodology, a master of science degree in industrial technology with an industrial safety concentration, and a bachelor of science degree in health and safety studies with an occupational safety and health education concentration. He is published widely in professional journals, including *The Journal of Safety Research* and *Professional Safety*. Dr. Janicak is a professional member of the American Society of Safety Engineers.

Christopher A. Janicak, PhD, CSP, ARM Professor of Safety
Indiana University of Pennsylvania
Indiana, PA 15705
cjanicak@iup.edu

43861482R00112

Made in the USA
Lexington, KY
15 August 2015